Sa

INTRODUCTI

DEDICATION	9
ACKNOWLEDGMENTS	11
CHAPTER 1	**13**
Uruguay	13
Preparations for the Trip	17
The Final Question	22
CHAPTER 2	**25**
The Trip	25
CHAPTER 3	**38**
First Time in Canada	38
The Sweet Wait	46
A Difficult Crossroads	47
CHAPTER 4	**52**
Life Without my Daughter	52
A Heartbreaking Visit	56
Patience, a Quality I Had Not Developed	59
CHAPTER 5	**61**
All Together in Canada	61
Our Big, Fat Jewish Wedding	69
CHAPTER 6	**74**
My First Work Steps	74
The Phone	79
First Visit of my Inspiring Muse	83
The Graduation	85
My Daughter Became My Teacher	87
CHAPTER 7	**91**
Growth	91

Say YES, Ask questions later

Another Great Mentor _____96
New Opportunities on the Horizon _____99
What is a Consultant? _____103
If I Could be Several Marianas! _____104
Alice, my Guardian Angel _____105
Be Different _____108

CHAPTER 8 _____112

More Growth _____112
Purses in my Kitchen. NO! _____114
The Giant Purse _____115
Alice and her Family _____122
Growing Pains _____127
The Real-Life Skills University _____129
The Academic World_____133
Fame and Ego _____136

CHAPTER 9 _____138

The Surgery _____138
An Angel Came into our Lives _____142
Hard News _____144
The Unexpected _____146
What Else Could Happen? _____152

CHAPTER 10 _____157

Be Part of the Community _____157
My God, this is Paradise!_____161
Fabulous at 50_____164
Self Esteem Doesn't Come in a Bottle_____168

CHAPTER 11 _____171

On Top of the Mountain _____171
The Body_____176
The Soul_____178
Christmas Party at Princess Florence _____181

CHAPTER 12 _____185

Change of Directions _____185

Save the Secret _____ 189

CHAPTER 13 _____ 194

The Sale _____ 194

CONCLUSION _____ 203

Why Tell My Story? _____ 203

Say YES,
Ask Questions Later

Opening YOUR Life to Opportunities

MARIANA KONSOLOS

Mariana Konsolos

Copyright © 2020 Mariana Konsolos
All rights reserved.
Vancouver, B.C. Canada
First English Edition
ISBN: 9781724140364

All rights reserved. No part of this publication may be reproduced, distributed, or transmitted in any form or by any means, including photocopying, recording, or other electronic or mechanical methods, including storage in a retrieval system, without the prior permission of the author and publisher.

The information contained in this book is for self-education purposes only and is not intended to provide specific advice to any individual.

Say YES, Ask questions later

INTRODUCTION

There were dark and painful moments when I left South America, to move to Edmonton, Canada. The temperature plummeted from 30 degrees above to 30 degrees below freezing. The shock was cruel. Being an immigrant was devastating. I didn't know the language; I didn't understand the culture. I didn't know how to navigate that new world. Perseverance and determination helped me not only survive but thrive.

Today's Coronavirus crisis is scary, but if YOU choose to shift your perspective, it can be a new canvas. This book is an invitation for YOU to seize the colourful supply of technological resources available to paint a better version of YOUR life and our world.

As with many people trapped in lockdown, I am wondering…Are YOU becoming more creative and resourceful in the light of adversity? Are YOU learning new techniques and tools to face the future better prepared?

The main question to YOU is straightforward:

"Are YOU going to take this opportunity or are you going to leave the canvas blank?"

Say YES, Ask questions later

DEDICATION

I dedicate this book to my daughter, the sunshine of my life. She is an incredible source of inspiration, knowledge, and happiness. She keeps me up to date! Her hard questions from a young age and her unique perspective about life molded me to think differently and deeper. She faced me up against new and valuable lessons that I would never have had encountered without her. She is a woman of strength and dignity, which makes me very proud of her. I am blessed and thankful for the gift of motherhood!

But let's be honest—this book wouldn't exist without Eli. He appeared in my life when I lost hope in love, life and freedom. He proved to me that true love exists, and it's worth every effort and sacrifice to find it. I feel very safe in his arms, the same as I felt the first time he hugged me twenty years ago. With his trust and support, I was able to allow myself to open up and offer the best of me to my family and the world.

My parents shaped me with all that they gave me and the things they didn't or couldn't. "Get moving if you want to see the melons settling in the cart," I can hear my mom saying. "Every woman needs to be financially independent. What are you doing to achieve that?" is another one that keeps playing in my mind more often than not.

How many times I find myself repeating my dad's sentences to my daughter, "Saving is the base of all fortunes," or "Owe money so you will have a good purpose to wake up in the morning."

The power of my parents' words is stronger than they can even imagine. Their words are stamped in my heart and will stay with me forever.

All I can feel is gratitude.

Say YES, Ask questions later

ACKNOWLEDGMENTS

Writing this book taught me some of the biggest lessons of my life—accepting the unknown with peace, and grace. To surrender without resistance.

Meeting Esmeralda Berbel, writer, was a blessing. She guided me into a journey of free flow, allowing me to pour my heart and life stories on paper in a safe and natural way.

My husband Eli, who is always a great sport when it comes to following my adventures: deciding to go to Barcelona with me and keep me in balance with healthy food, walks, cultural life, and relaxing times at the beach.

I want to thank Shaun Fitzpatrick, former Airbnb host the first time we came to Vancouver, and today, a very close friend of our family, who had generously offered his time to review the very first translation of my book. He was amazing trying to interpret my "translations from Spanish" using his wisdom and wit.

Kelly Falardeau championed me offering her unconditional support, encouragement, wise advice, and recommending me to a highly skilled professional, Patricia Pysyk Ogilvie. Thank you also to Pam Robertson Rivet who helped me edit and format the book.

Lastly, I want to thank my dear Dianna Bowes who was helping me to finalize this project, designing my

Say YES, Ask questions later

cover page, and making some adjustments to the overall look of the book. Unfortunately, health issues interrupted us many times in the past years and have now been truncated forever by her recent passing. Even though it was hard, I decided to finalize and publish the book to honor Dianna by spreading and amplifying the values and messages we shared on a very deep level.

Thank you to all the women and men I met throughout the years: customers, employees, employers, teachers, and mentors who shaped me into the person I am today.

CHAPTER 1

Uruguay

It was 1999 and I was living in Punta del Este, better known as the French Riviera of South America. I was seen as a successful young entrepreneur by colleagues and customers. Despite the luxurious lifestyle I was living, my soul felt unsettled and empty. Even the financial success I was experiencing, strong and limiting family unspoken mandates prevented me from enjoying true freedom.

I suffered a spine injury that changed everything. I decided to take a sabbatical for an entire year. A month in hospital made me realize that the business worked without me. Suddenly I understood that I was not essential, and that time was running relentlessly. My daughter was already five years old and memories of crossing the street with her to enjoy the beach were too few and far between.

Now I felt I had the time to ask myself all the questions I had never asked myself, "Where was I going? What was I looking for? Why? What for?" I found no answers.

Since my divorce when my daughter was only ten months old, all I had done was work to achieve my long-awaited financial independence. I was convinced, since I was very young, that only then would I be free to live in accordance with my values

Say YES, Ask questions later

and desires. I would no longer have to give explanations to my family or the rest of the world.

But, four years after conquering the famous Everest of financial autonomy, I still could not feel the freedom.

I remember that day in mid-September, I arrived home as the sun was setting. The sky had been painted the color of fire. The sea was calm. A spring wind stroked my hair as I stepped out onto the terrace where I was planning to work for a few hours.

I opened my computer and immediately the "hu-hu" of the ICQ rang, I am not sure if you remember it! It was the first instant digital messaging service ever. The cute logo was a green flower that would change color when someone was online. It was the very beginning of the Internet era in Uruguay and I had challenged myself to learn new technologies to advance my business.

"Shalom!" appeared on my screen.

I looked at the name of the person who sent the communication and did not recognize it. "Do I know you?" I typed.

"No, you do not know me," he replied. "Sorry to bother you, but I would like to travel to South America, and I need some tips." He continued. "I live in Canada even though I was born in Istanbul and moved to Israel at thirteen. I travelled all over the world, but I have never been to the southern hemisphere."

Mariana Konsolos

We wrote to each other for three hours that day. This intruder without a face and without a voice made me curious to know more about him. I felt there was something to discover, something that particularly attracted me to this man named Eli.

The conversations became more frequent throughout the coming days. They were in Hebrew, written phonetically with the Latin alphabet. Remember! At the time there was no way to speak or see each other. Each time we met online, the stories became deeper and more interesting. We discovered we had much in common: the passion for travel, gastronomy, family, divorce, daughters and work. In all the conversations, our respective daughters were the priority. That gave me an important sense of tranquility.

Weeks and months passed, and the relationship became closer despite the distance. As time passed by, we found new ways to communicate. We bought microphones and discovered programs that allowed us to listen to each other's voices. All this was very innovative for that time, incredibly only twenty years ago.

His accent was a mixture of Ladino (old Spanish of Jewish Sephardic immigrants), English and Hebrew, and carried a special charm. His voice was calm and confident. During those months we shared joys that happened to us with our respective daughters, fights

Say YES, Ask questions later

with our former partners, work and family problems. We learned to listen, to advise and to support each other from a distance. Slowly we started to spend more and more hours chatting, but it never seemed enough.

My days were spent doing mom tasks and learning voraciously the new technology that would allow me to serve my customers from around the world better. But when nighttime came and after my little girl had fallen asleep, I settled myself on a mattress that I had positioned next to the computer in the living room (the computer was attached to the phone line as wireless was not in existence), and our online romance resumed.

My friends still remember and laugh at this funny scene. We began to plan our first face-to-face meeting. It was already October, and February was the date chosen to meet in Cuba, a destination neither of us knew. It sounded exotic, funny and—why deny it—super romantic.

One afternoon in late November, frustrated by so many conversations interrupted by the bad internet signal, I told Eli that I could not keep waiting and 'dating with a computer screen'. He, calm as always, told me that he felt the same way. Despite that he couldn't advance the trip because it was the busiest time in the taxi business, and he could not afford to miss that income.

I liked his security, his clear priorities, the conversation without turns or pretensions. Very spontaneously I told him that I could go, since I was still on my sabbatical year, and I also could afford it financially. Without hesitation and with the joy that characterizes him, he answered, "Come whenever you want; here you are always welcome."

Preparations for the Trip

As preparations began, opinions from family and friends soon followed. My parents were convinced that I had a loose screw in my head. First, the sabbatical year, then, an online date, and to top it up, traveling to meet him in Canada. "What the hell is she thinking?"

My girlfriends had a special 'witches' meeting to discuss the topic of my trip. Alby, the most skeptical in the group, said, "I don't know; this is not right. Think about it Mariana, it's dangerous. What if he's crazy or a serial killer? Oh, God, I'm going to light candles to the Virgin of Rosario to protect you."

Gaby, the most liberal and an atheist said, "Life is short. Go meet him and enjoy! What is the worst that can happen?"

Another friend, trapped in a dependent relationship, threatened, "If you leave, I'll never talk to you again. It's not right to leave everything behind to go after a man."

Say YES, Ask questions later

I saw with clarity how everyone of them was projecting their own fears and values on my trip. But my heart was calm. After hearing all the opinions and prejudices of the people around me, my instincts told me YES. I felt that I had to go, that it was worth it to take some chances. I purchased my ticket. November 28 was my departure date and after that I started to become nervous!

By then, I had befriended some of Eli's friends online. This gave me the opportunity to become a self-styled private investigator. I asked each of them the same questions and then compared their answers to see if they matched. Yes, everything seemed to be right and would go smooth. Eli started to get excited, and yet despite that, my insecurities and fears started to surface.

In each daily talk I made sure to tell him that I was fat, that he shouldn't expect a model, nor a Barbie doll, because I was not. I was afraid. What if he did not like me? What if I did not like him? What if there was no chemistry between us? My lack of self-esteem was playing tricks on me.

At long last the day before my trip was at hand. I was at the spa receiving the royal treatment: massage, hair removal, color, manicure, pedicure and eyebrows for an all new look when my travel agent called to tell me that he had missed an important detail. To travel to Canada, Uruguayans would need a visa.

"Visa? And today you tell me?" I asked indignantly. "What should I do?"

He replied that if I made a stop in Buenos Aires, the Canadian Consulate would issue the visa overnight, and he would change my flight to Canada for the next day. I had no choice but to accept.

I immediately called Eli to tell him the news. After ringing three times, my call was answered by an unknown male voice, "Hello?"

I hung up and dialed the number again. I told myself, "I must have dialed wrong."

But to my surprise, the same voice answered again, "Hello?"

In my faltering English I asked for Eli. He told me Eli was working and gave me Eli's cell phone number. I wondered who this person was. Eli had never mentioned him.

Concerned, I dialed the number that the mysterious voice had given me and again the same person answered. I hung up on him. Now I was disconcerted. The hours passed and Eli did not call me back. I began to distrust him.

That afternoon felt eternal, and as the hours passed, I was getting angrier. I entered a state of trance. The most macabre and dark stories emerged from the depth of my frightened mind. All my fears mingled with the latest horror movies I had seen on television, and the combination was scary. Could he be a member of a trafficking network? Is he a sexual

Say YES, Ask questions later

predator or organ trader? I was very angry with myself not finding out more. I reproached myself for such naivety.

The ring, ring of the phone brought me out of my reverie. It was Eli, with a calm and serene voice. As if by magic, the bad thoughts evaporated.

"Who answered your phone?" I asked, with a mixture of hostility and curiosity.

"It was Gerry, Gerry Dallas," he said quietly.

"And who is Gerry Dallas?" I persisted.

"Gerry is my tenant. Rents a room in my house. He's lived with me for eight years."

I was irritated by his casual indifference, and I continued asking. "Why did you never tell me? What else are you hiding from me? Why did he answer me at both numbers?"

With total serenity, he continued, "I forgot my cell phone at home. Gerry works at night; I hardly see him. When I arrive, he leaves and when I leave, he returns. I didn't think it was important."

How could he not have considered it an important piece of information? How had he not thought to tell me anything about it? Would there be more secrets?

He challenged me, "If you don't trust me, better not come. If everything is going to be a scandal, we'd better leave it here."

"Scandal?" I reacted. I was outraged and answered with an ironic tone, "You are right. I'm not going anywhere!"

"Well, as you wish," he answered calmly as always.

I felt hurt. I cut the communication and abruptly ended the call.

I cried and cried. I felt a mixture of anger, sadness and impotence. The dream of so many months had escaped through my fingers like water. I did not understand what had happened. As the hours passed, slowly I calmed down. I knew I had to make a decision, and soon, because my flight was scheduled for the next day. My options were few and clear. Either cancel the ticket or give this dream another chance. "After all, what was hidden from me is not so important," an inner voice told me. "But he hid it from you," another voice reminded me. I resolved to call him and talk a little more before deciding.

"Hello! Are you calmer?" Eli asked me as soon as he answered the phone.

"Yes," I said. "I don't like lies because they make me very scared."

"But I didn't lie to you. I didn't tell you something because I didn't believe it was relevant."

I believed him. I knew he was an honest man. I realized that it was part of his life and that it didn't really make any difference in our relationship. I finally shared the news about arriving a day later because of the visa issue. Our conversation got animated once again. We spoke of the travel plans and the last-minute preparations for the trip. We laughed together about Gerry. Everything went back to normal. I was again at peace with myself and with the decision to go.

The Final Question

Near the end of the conversation, he asked permission to ask me a difficult question. Again, my heart was compressed.

With shyness and some hesitation, he asked me, "You told me more than once that you're not skinny, that you're chubby, that I should not expect a model, that you're not a Barbie. When you say 'chubby', do you mean ... a ... chubby chubby? Or.... a little chubby?" And without a second thought, he launched the question like a dart, "Do you occupy one or two places on the plane?"

I started to laugh out loud! I found his honesty incredible with such a touch of almost childlike ingenuity. I thought to myself, "A Latino man would never have asked that question." I liked his style very much, so fresh and spontaneous. "Yes," I thought, "we're going to get along." Overcome with laughter, I answered that he should stay calm for I would be occupying just a single airplane seat.

That night I could not sleep. I was anxious about the events of that day and thousands of thoughts were spinning in my head. I pondered the last telephone conversation and realized the terrible body image I had of myself. I was an attractive woman; plump and curvaceous. And very sexy! But the way I described myself to Eli during all those months over the telephone made him believe I was so big and fat that I would occupy two seats on the plane. I portrayed myself as an obese person because, in my mind, I felt and saw myself as obese.

In Uruguay finding clothes for my size was not easy. The sizes were very small, and the options limited. My mom would say, "You're not going to find a boyfriend; men like the thin ones." And that was the only reality in which I was submerged for many years. For the same reason, fashion accessories had been my best friends for years: dressed in basic colors, with the help of a purse, a pair of shoes or an interesting scarf I knew how to create different looks. As a good 'chubby,' I had the grace to dress well.

My mother had suffered from being overweight in her youth. Fearing the same would happen to me, she was obsessed with it. In my house there was never much food. My friends laughed when they opened our refrigerator because there was only lettuce, tomatoes, jelly, and maybe another vegetable. My brother and I loved to visit friends or neighbors where there were

Say YES, Ask questions later

always good cakes or delicious schnitzels, delicacies that were not allowed in our house.

It amuses me to remember when at the table, we all carefully ate the "right amounts" as mom was watching us over her glasses. But at night, when she was sleeping, my brother, my dad and I not-so-accidentally found ourselves in the kitchen pecking in a half-empty refrigerator. Today I think it was tragicomic, but that was the only reality we learned at home.

I felt for many years that I was never thin enough in her eyes. Today, after so many years, when I see old photos of myself, I realize that I allowed my mother's distorted vision to define my own body image.

And so, with Eli's witty question in mind, I fell asleep, smiling and satisfied that the next day I would get on the plane that would take me to meet the mysterious human being who broke into my thoughts and exalted my emotions.

More importantly, I would occupy a single airplane seat!

CHAPTER 2

The Trip

Early the next morning, I flew to Buenos Aires and went directly to the Canadian Embassy to handle the visa process. In the afternoon I could go back to pick up my passport with the required visa, and the following morning, if everything went well, I would be ready to travel.

At noon I was having lunch with Sandra and Denise, my Argentine childhood friends who used to come to Punta del Este every summer. They wanted to know all the details of my new adventure and the man who was the main character of the story I was about to live.

I told them I conjured up several plans including an escape option. If I arrived at the airport, saw him and did not like something about him or felt somehow insecure, I would ignore him and pass by. I would then rent a car and travel on alone. I could do that simply enough, because he did not know me. He had seen only one picture of me. It was the only one I managed to send after many months of frustrated attempts. I confess that I intentionally sent him a terrible picture of me, one of the ugliest that I had. Why? Because I did not want him to connect with me just because of my physical appearance. I cared about our connection beyond physical attraction.

On the other hand, if I liked what I saw but still didn't feel completely safe, I would accept an offer to travel with him, but only on the condition we stayed overnight in separate rooms. That way, I would be free to escape in case of emergency. If I loved his looks and the chemistry between us was amazing, and if I felt safe, I would agree to travel with him to Jasper and Banff for a week, as friends. If something romantic developed beyond friendship, and if we both agreed, we could head back to Edmonton, where he would show me his house and introduce me to his daughter and his friends. It seemed like a solid plan.

The girls were excited listening to the story. From time to time, they interrupted me, adding humorous touches and erotic ideas. We laughed like little girls mixing nerves and complicity.

They lived through a winter season in Germany and knew what snow could mean. I was overrun by questions such as, "Are you taking long pants, warm shoes, adequate clothes for thirty degrees below zero?"

Of course, the answer to every concern was, "No!"

They warned me that there could be a snowstorm and the roads could be difficult to travel. Therefore, if I arrived at the airport and Eli was not there, I should wait an extra hour to give him time to arrive, allowing for any climatic eventuality. They begged me not to drive in the mountains, as it was very difficult, and I did not have any experience in that environment. All this clearly showed the degree of unconsciousness, naiveté and irresponsibility I had. I was so excited to meet Eli that I had not considered any of those details. Blessed are the friends who think for us! Later that afternoon I picked up my passport with the Canadian Visa. Now I was ready for the trip!

*****

I sat on the plane. I was so tired. The stress of the past few days took its toll on me. My trip would be twenty-four hours, counting a stop in Chicago, and I hoped to get some sleep. I tried to fall asleep, but my thoughts did not let me. My mind wandered far back in time. I thought about my parents. How many successes and how many failures they had endured? Both came from very humble Polish Jewish immigrant families who had come to Uruguay to escape the war in Europe.

As a young man, my dad applied himself. He was responsible and a very good student. Thanks to the help of some scholarships from his school in Pando, a city on the outskirts of Montevideo where his family lived, some weekend jobs, and the efforts of his father, a local barber, he managed to study at the University of the Republic and become a Public Accountant, the pride of his family!

Say YES, Ask questions later

My mother lost her father, a carpenter, when she was very young, and had to leave school in order to help her mother maintain the house. She was an intuitive, curious young woman, full of life, dreams and big ambitions. Her ideas were always innovative, and she possessed an innate good taste and refined aesthetic sense.

Shortly after they first met, my parents got married and had two children: my brother Marcelo and me. My father, as an accomplished accountant and the son of immigrants, had learned that saving was the basis of fortune. Thus, with his first salaries, he managed to save enough money to buy a piece of land and pay for it in installments. His intention was to build a house on the land and then resell it. My mom chose a lot near a school, because she said there would always be a young family with school-age children and money to buy.

"You always have to owe money," my dad said, "so there will always be a good reason to get up and work every morning." With lots of effort my parents managed to save enough money to build a modest house on the land. My mom had been right. The closeness to the school was a great asset for a young family and the house was sold as soon as it was finished. So, they continued building, each time a bigger house, in a better location, a nicer layout.

After a few years, my mother became interested in a resort town, Punta del Este, where the rich and famous went to escape and play. She suggested that their next land should be bought there. So, it was. They were a perfect team. My dad managed the money and my mom had the intuition to pick the best locations and design the most amazing houses. Her good taste grew refined over time.

There were no interior design magazines that she did not look at in order to come up with ideas. She was simply a genius! In the early years, for lack of sufficient resources, she bought inexpensive furniture at auctions and recycled them. She knew how to choose unique pieces and had a team of artisans transforming them according to her fertile imagination; her ideas were inspired by the furnishings of the French castles in the Loire Valley.

People soon recognized her at auctions because she invested in items that nobody dared to buy. Seeing a dresser that by its height could not enter current houses, she imagined how to transform it in creative ways. From the top she could make a mantle for the fireplace, the mirror would serve for the bathroom, the lower part for the main dining room. In addition, since the Carrara marble top was too beautiful to be left on the sideboard, it would be better used for the kitchen counter. It could be replaced by a patinated wooden top to make the piece look old. It was fascinating to see her create! Her eyes lit up and her passion overflowed. She was really happy and fulfilled.

Say YES, Ask questions later

My dad paid the bills, negotiated the prices and stopped mom when she wanted to buy everything she saw. 'Eva's homes' as they were known over time in the market, were a true seal of quality and good taste in the exclusive real estate market in Punta del Este!

"But everything comes with a price tag." I thought to myself. My parents' success, all those years of hard work and passionate dedication, kept them away from us. Slowly they were staying away for longer periods in Punta del Este, and my brother and I spent most of our time with my maternal grandmother Mina, in Montevideo, Uruguay's major metropolis and capital city.

Abu Mina, as we called her, had survived the Second World War thanks to her wit and street smarts. She said 'yes' to any job, even if she did not know how to do it, hoping to learn it in order to at least eat and be warm for a day. Each day that she survived was one more day that she shortchanged death. Her curiosity knew no bounds. She read everything that came into her hands. If it was in another language, she learned it. They said that in Poland her father sent her to work and she escaped at night to study and be an activist with the Communists Party. Before leaving Poland for the long sailing to Uruguay, she purchased a Polish-Spanish dictionary and studied intensely during the passage. When they arrived at the Rio de la Plata, she was speaking almost perfect Spanish.

Mariana Konsolos

My brother was Abu's great companion. Close with her, he acquired a great passion for reading. As a shy and introverted child, he enjoyed going to Punta del Este on weekends to spend time with my parents. There he could read endlessly and not be bothered by other children who insisted on going out to play soccer, which he didn't care about in the least. On the other hand, I was very social and always had my calendar full of commitments in Montevideo, especially during the weekend. That's why I hated going to Punta del Este when my parents forced me to go. Their insistence made me lose out on the activities of the youth organization to which I belonged. Over the years, I became a youth organization's community leader. Through it, at seventeen, I traveled to Israel for the first time, an experience that marked my life forever.

Unfortunately, my parents were not often present during my adolescence, the years when I needed them most. Slowly I learned to find my way alone. I became more and more independent. My parents wanted to be there, but they couldn't. Their work absorbed them and at the same time they loved it. Sometimes they called us to say, "We will be leaving in an hour from Punta del Este; we will be in Montevideo for lunch." That hour transformed into several hours, and sometimes into days. We learned not to wait for them, not to believe in promises, because they never fulfilled them. At week's end, our

Say YES, Ask questions later

Abu didn't know what to cook for us with the few things that were left in the refrigerator.

My friends became my family of life. With them I shared everything: my first kiss, high school exams, failures with boys, conflicts with friends. Sunday was the hardest day of the week for me. While everyone had lunch as a family, I was alone. I learned to sleep late to avoid feeling the loneliness that hurt so much. The only good thing about it was that I did not have time induced deadlines to meet when I went out at night. I was absolutely free.

*****

"What would you like to drink?" the stewardess asked, jolting me back to the present and interrupting my thoughts.

"Wine, please," I answered. Maybe that will help me sleep, I thought. I needed to rest, since there would be hectic days ahead.

I ate my dreary airplane dinner and imagined my daughter having dinner alone with Ana, the lady who takes care of her. To think that she was already five years old! We lived along the seashore and yet we did not go to the beach because I thought I was fat. How had I missed so many opportunities to enjoy the beach and its wonders because of my own insecurities? Would anyone remember the opportunities I had wasted: the times I could have been making sandcastles with my little girl, to jump in the waves and play in the ocean until sunset? Nobody would remember it. It was only years later, when I met Kelly, that I regretted not having understood what was really important. Sometimes I wish I would have known that I was not the center of the world and nobody was watching or caring about me, my shape, or my size.

I must admit that in the years that followed my divorce, my life had been an absolute mess. I had been so busy trying to meet the financial goals I imposed on myself that I had neglected the rest. I worked hard and endless hours to indulge myself and my daughter with exotic trips and a luxurious lifestyle. Unfortunately, I did not follow my dad's advice; I wasn't saving for the future. I would go out from time to time on dates to fill my loneliness, to recover the self-esteem lost in the years of my marriage. I bought a house and made major renovations by assuming a big mortgage. A year later the real estate market collapsed, and I could not afford it and lost the place. I was not finding peace with myself.

That's when I decided to take care of myself. I had to stop smoking, as I was smoking three packages a day, lose weight and lower my stress levels. I went to Vida Sana, a spiritual center in Argentina where I had been years ago. Here was a place where I could let go and be pampered and cared for as much as I wanted. But what I did not imagine was that after a week, as soon as I lowered all my resistances and let myself be taken care of, my body would scream, "Enough!"

The body spoke and usually does but sadly we are not always ready to listen to it. We believe that we must be super women with special powers. We believe that we can work without limits, be good moms, impeccable ladies, excellent sisters, incredible daughters, outstanding entrepreneurs and unbeatable friends. My body shouted, "Enough!"

At the retreat I was attacked by a terrible lumbago that tightened my sciatic nerve and left me absolutely immobile. I was flown back to Uruguay where, arriving in a wheelchair, I was taken directly to a hospital and stayed for one long month.

Life had given me a slap in the face, showing me that there are no certainties. I did not know if I was going to walk again, but the world continued its course quite nicely without me. Nobody and nothing stops. I discovered abruptly that I was not a superwoman, nor was I essential. I was a simple human being, and without health I was nothing. The only one who really needed me, and her world would crumble if anything happened to me, was my beloved and only daughter.

*****

I had drifted off to sleep, but turbulence woke me. I felt confused and did not know when I had fallen asleep. Evidently the wine had helped. I looked at the clock. Four hours were missing. I settled in and kept on sleeping. I woke up when we landed in Chicago. Now everything felt very real. In a few hours Eli and I would be together.

I got off the plane and looked for the boarding gate to Edmonton. And to think that six months ago I did not know that a city with that name existed! It never occurred to me to travel to Canada. All I did was work and work. So much time passed, so many experiences, how many achievements in so few years! But how much effort? How many hours of work and dedication? Some failure experiences came to my mind, and I realized they were not by coincidence the ones that taught me the most.

I remembered the day a gentleman with a strong accent, a mixture of Polish and Spanish from Bolivia, entered my office for the first time. He sat at the desk in front of me and said, "My name is Jacobo. I am an investor and I only look for opportunities. Do you have any?"

I said, "Yes," convincingly, even though I had no clue what I was about to offer him. I got his information and a week later I told him about some land where I saw a great future. Don Jacobo bought it! He really believed in me. He perceived more potential in me than I had seen in myself. Over the coming years he gave me the opportunity to learn how to work real estate with real money and big risks. He

Say YES, Ask questions later

taught me how to separate feelings from business and accept that to lose is part of the game. He taught me to see opportunities where nobody would and never to be afraid to go against the grain. If everyone bought, he sold. If everyone sold, he bought. He always had a capital fund that he used to bet. And he bet on young people, with new ideas; he bet on things he did not understand but in which he had confidence. He was of the old guard, of those persons who believed in giving your word with an honorable handshake.

Over the years I learned that Don Jacobo had his investments dispersed in different markets throughout the world. That gray-haired man, with the identification number of the concentration camp tattooed on his right arm, as my mother would say, was definitely a very powerful man. But, despite his economic power, he was a man with a special sensitivity. I suspect that because he had survived the Holocaust, he saw the world through a different lens, a different paradigm than did my parents. He knew how to enjoy life! He loved to travel and, as soon as he could afford it, he began to invite his childhood friends who had also survived the war to visit Argentina, where he lived the last years of his life.

For some friends, he paid their ticket, for others, their stay. He travelled to Europe many times to visit and spend time with them. His wife explained to me that those friends were like real brothers. With them, he lived the most absolute misery and had seen the most frightful horrors of war. They held onto a reservoir of shared stories, and in each meeting, they remembered and repeated them. She explained that it was kind of a therapy, a catharsis that freed them from the nightmares and traumas that other survivors could not overcome.

Don Jacobo told me many times he survived by chance, he learned how to negotiate to eat, how he saw many friends and family die, and how at the end of the war, he was thirteen years old and weighed thirty kilos. Many times, I wanted to ask permission to record the stories he told me, and I did not do it for fear of offending him. Today I regret it because, when I miss him, I would love to be able to enjoy the stories I learned from him. He was a great teacher to me; he was like the grandfather I never met.

The call came through the loudspeakers to board for Edmonton. What a thrill! At last, in a few hours, I was going to meet Eli in person.

CHAPTER 3

First Time in Canada

The plane landed in a city covered in white. I have never seen so much snow in my life. My heart was beating hard. Now I was truly afraid! What if he did not come? What if I did not like him? There was no time for regrets.

I took my purse, pulled out my makeup bag, painted my lips, dabbed perfume, and combed my hair. I gathered courage and got up from my seat to walk the aisle of the plane as if it was the runway of a fashion show.

In the airport, my suitcase arrived right away. And finally, I went out. It was cold. I looked and looked around and Eli was not there. I remembered the advice of my friends from Buenos Aires. Maybe a snowstorm had delayed him. I sat inside the airport, near the door of the arrivals, and picked up a booklet that I found next to me. I tried to read it, but I couldn't focus. Again, the fears. I had to think what I would do in case he did not arrive in the next hour. I tried again to distract myself by reading the booklet. Suddenly, I looked up and there he was, with a smile that lit up his face.

Eli was just as I had imagined him. He apologized, "I arrived early and went up for a coffee to pass the time. Your flight landed earlier than expected and it was never announced. Please forgive me!" It was an odd situation: we knew each other, but we did not know each other. We were not sure how to act or how to greet each other. It was obvious we were both nervous.

"Don't worry," I said. "Hola! I am glad to finally be here; it was a long trip!" and promptly kissed his cheek just like we do in Uruguay. He gave me a kiss too, although later I learned that in Canada people normally shake hands.

He took my luggage and said, "Let's go! We have many places to visit today." When we got to the car, he placed my suitcase in the trunk and, once seated, took my hand and kissed it saying very seriously. "You are much prettier than I imagined, and not fat at all. I'm happy you're here with me. Thanks for coming! I'll make this trip the most beautiful one you've ever had in your life."

In that same moment I began to fall in love with the man who made me experience absolute peace. I was totally attracted to Eli's open smile and his immediate transparency. His strong muscular arms made me wish he'd hug me to feel protected. Suddenly, I realized that I had not been taken care of for many years.

Say YES, Ask questions later

I longed for that feeling; I wanted desperately to be given affection and emotional containment. I realized that I had reached far away to Canada with the dream that this calm-faced man could give me what I needed so badly.

We drove past landscapes of beautiful snowy mountains. Slowly we resumed the talks that we had begun so many times that were interrupted by a choppy Internet. We felt like old friends who had not seen each other for a long time. We were very comfortable with each other.

As he excitedly shared the itinerary he had planned, I got distracted thinking about the details Eli had taken into account. He bought me a phone card, so I could call my daughter and my parents and tell them I had arrived safely. "Who does that?" I thought. He also presented me with my favorite chocolates, a fact that I had mentioned some time ago in our online chats. I could not believe he had remembered!

I returned to pay attention to the conversation, and after listening to the tour we would do together I proposed I share the expenses of the trip. He categorically denied the offer. "You paid the ticket to Canada and the rest would be on me," he announced. I was not accustomed to this kind of man. Nobody had ever paid anything for me. How strange and how nice to be his guest. I was thrilled by this novice experience.

After spending the day enjoying the mountains and visiting places I only saw on postcards, night fell, and we arrived at the hotel. What would happen now? Had he booked a single room or two? In the lobby he asked me if I would feel comfortable sharing the room. I accepted timidly, but inside it was what I most wanted. We entered the room, and when the door closed there was a moment of uncomfortable silence. He approached me. With his strong hands he gently held my face, looked at me for a moment and kissed me. It was a tender and passionate kiss. It was a magical moment that lasted a long time. Neither of us wanted it to end. This was the moment we both had dreamed of for so many months.

This attraction knew no tiredness, fears or embarrassment. We drank wine and ate chocolate in the bathtub. Between talks and kisses, Eli did something that nobody had ever done before; he kissed my feet. This man knew how to love from head to toe.

Despite my difficulty falling asleep while being hugged by someone, both of us felt rested and intertwined for the full night. It definitely felt good. I fell asleep thinking of my life as a puzzle that lost a piece for years. That night I felt I found the missing piece. Eli, from Canada, fit perfectly into my puzzle.

The whole trip felt like a dream. I experienced the magnificent Rocky Mountains accompanied by this warm and funny man who made me laugh as I hadn't in years.

Walking through Banff, sipping delicious warming coffees infused with Baileys at Lake Louise, lunch at Jasper Park Lodge, and dipping into the hot springs at Radium, we stripped our souls and brought our hearts closer. We shared family stories, travel memories and dreams of everything we wanted to do over the next few years of our lives.

And there he was. Divorced ten years, living near his adored daughter, working from sunrise to sunset to assure them both a future. I found this wonderful man on the internet from the other side of the world! How could this be explained? How could it be that nobody all these years had discovered him? Could it be that I was so lucky?

After a week together, thousands of hours of conversations, and lots of laughter, he suggested that we head back to Edmonton and I get to know his home, his daughter and his friends. The plan worked in the best way that could be expected.

His house was small, simple and very cozy. The absence of a female hand was noticeable. Nothing was missing, but if I wanted to set the table for four people, there were not four glasses that matched. I closed my eyes and I could dream it decorated and full of color. I could see myself living here despite the snow on the streets and the simplicity of the life that Eli could offer me.

That night we were invited for dinner at the home of one of his friends. I was nervous. Would they accept me? I dressed up and put on makeup. I asked Eli his opinion, "Do I look good?"

He laughed and said, "You better change. You're very cute, but too provocative for Edmonton." That was what I liked most about him: always honest and without games, straightforward, without Latin hysterics.

I knew how to adapt. I changed clothing and we left. It was cold with lots of snow. Upon arriving, Eli told me that I had to take off my shoes, a habit I did not know. What a shame! My stockings did not match my outfit. "Important things to remember for the next time," I thought. Everyone received us very cheerfully. You could tell Eli was loved by these people a lot. "They must have been worried too," I mused. They were probably thinking, "Who could be that mysterious woman who came from South America to meet Eli? What interests does she have?"

I was glued to him. They all spoke the Hebrew language which I had not practiced for years. It was hard for me to understand them, maybe because I was nervous. Some tried to speak to me in basic Spanish, but, truthfully, they did not know much. They were lovely, but they were investigating me. Who was I? What was my job? With whom had I left my daughter? Who did I work for? Would I move to Canada? I felt I was going through an examination to

Say YES, Ask questions later

see if I was the woman for Eli. At the end of the night, I felt that I had passed the exam. They had approved of me and they were willing to welcome me if I decided to move to Canada.

Returning to Eli's home, we laughed at their questions, concerns and the unfiltered comments from some of the women in the group. Eli shared the individual stories of each who were at the get-together. He elaborated on how he met them and his relationships with them. They were the closest people to him, those with whom he spent holidays and birthdays. That night I felt like I had been introduced to his family and I had passed the test, which made both of us feel happy.

Every day more walls fell that had separated us. For many years we both lived inside strong walls meant to protect ourselves. We were becoming closer, but at the same time more vulnerable. It was scary.

The next day we picked up his daughter Rebecca from school. Eli adored her, and it showed. His eyes lit up when he saw her, and his tone of voice became very tender as he called her sweetie. I brought her typical Uruguayan gifts: *alfajores*, *dulce de leche*, a hand-knitted wool sweater and our traditional music. She appreciated the gifts. Rebecca was a really beautiful girl, with big turquoise eyes, blond hair and an angelic face. She was nine years old, quiet and more reserved than girls of her age in Uruguay. She was very respectful at all times but remained distant.

She did not play, nor did she chat much with me. Usually I got along very well with the children, but at that time I did not know how to approach her. "I will have to earn her trust," I thought. We ate together and then she danced ballet for us. Later we took her to the zoo and then back to her mom. According to Eli, the visit had been very positive. Rebecca had dared to dance in front of me.

And so, the days went by. Eli shared his life, his city, his favorite places, his customs, his daughter and his friends with me. I enjoyed every minute of the visit.

I liked the order, the calm and what I could observe of Canadian society. The snow did not bother me as much as I had imagined. And, of course, we started talking about the future. We tried to imagine what it would be like to live together, what I could do and work at in Canada. And so, full of hopes and dreams, with dozens of adventures experienced with Eli and as in love as a teenager, I went back to Uruguay happy and loved, but, above all things, with the strong feeling of being well cared for.

The Sweet Wait

During the months that followed we planned our next visit. This time it would be in Uruguay, where I could show him my world and introduce him to my loved ones. We continued to communicate online,

Say YES, Ask questions later

sharing our stories, on an internet that now offered facial and voice communication.

Eli came to Uruguay three months after I returned from Canada. He met my five-year-old daughter, my family and my friends. They adored him. He fell in love with my country and its culture. After traveling together through South America for two months, sharing, enjoying, laughing, learning about each other, and fighting, it was time to separate.

When he was about to leave, I asked him, "Now what?"

And with the same honesty as always, he answered, "Now I need to go back and see what I feel, see if I miss you." I felt that my world was crumbling. I was in love with Eli and I had nothing more to think about. I was willing to leave everything behind and move to snowy Edmonton to start a new life with him. I felt in my heart that I found the love of my life, and Eli was telling me that he was not sure and that he wanted to think about it. Then I felt apart.

Eli left.

The days went by and I entered into a generalized apathy. I looked after my daughter as best I could. I would get up to take her to school and then come back to bed again. Luckily, I had Ana who cooked, washed clothes and cleaned the house. I had no interest in anything or anyone. I did not see the light at the end of the tunnel. I did not understand what happened.

Why did Eli not choose me? What was it that he had to think about?

I was more discontented with the world than ever. The fights with my parents increased, and disagreements became unbearable with my ex. I wanted to go! I wanted a break! I wanted someone to love me without conditions or doubts!

A Difficult Crossroads

Depression was taking over me. The sciatic nerve in my back started to bother me again. I rarely left my house. I never went online or talked to Eli. My daughter moved in with her dad after a bitter fight we had. I slowly isolated myself completely. I did not want to talk to anyone, not my parents nor my friends. I was very angry with the world. I was not interested in anything.

Later I learned that during these difficult times, Eli tried unsuccessfully to communicate with me. He did manage to contact my parents. After learning what was happening to me, he boarded the first plane. Less than a month after leaving, he returned to Uruguay. He thought it over. He wanted to start his life with me, and he came to look for me. I felt ashamed of myself. Who would want me like that? Who could want to start a new life with a depressed person? I did not deserve anyone! He was too much for me!

I spoke with my ex-husband and told him that Eli came to take me to Canada with him and I wanted to

Say YES, Ask questions later

take my daughter with me. He told me, "Good for you! But my daughter is not going anywhere." Again, my heart broke. I did not want to leave her.

Eli was in Uruguay for ten days and helped me slowly recover. He patiently cared for me day and night. We went for walks, he fed me, he spoiled me, he told me stories about his trips, and he made me laugh often. This wonderful man understood how badly I was doing and suggested that he take me to Canada to continue caring for me until I recovered or until I felt strong enough to decide if I wanted to return to Uruguay. I knew it was a good idea, but that meant leaving my daughter. I couldn't imagine my life without her. I was at a difficult crossroad. I insisted on taking her with me. It didn't make any sense to me that my daughter would stay with her father's girlfriend, as he was working in Argentina and spending only weekends in Uruguay. My opinion caused fights with my ex which turned more combative than ever. The poor girl was in the middle of a fierce battle.

I am not a religious person, but one morning I woke up remembering this story I learned in grade six.

Once upon a time there were two women who had each given birth to beautiful baby boys. When one woman's son died, the grieving woman exchanged him for the living son of the other woman. The deception was not effective, and both claimed the living child as their son. They took the baby before King Solomon, who was said to be a very righteous governor. After hearing each other's story, he ordered his soldier: "Split the living child in two. Give half to one and the other half to the other."

When the soldier raised his sword, the one woman shouted, "Please, my Lord. Give her the child. Do not kill him." King Solomon took the baby in his arms and handed it to that same woman who had willingly relinquished her son despite her aching disappointment. Only a true mother would prefer to renounce her son rather than see him dead.

For me it was like a revelation. I should not keep fighting over my daughter. I understood that the only way to keep her safe and in one piece, was to accept leaving her with her father. I needed to accept the fact that I was extremely weak and trust her dad would take good care of her. I needed somebody to take care of me, so I could recover. I was tested to follow what I always claimed to be my top values: love and freedom.

And so, with a broken heart, I left for Canada with Eli and left my daughter for her father to take care of her. It was the saddest and hardest moment of my life.

The only thing I did the following weeks was cry and sleep. I felt very guilty about leaving my daughter, but also was angry at myself for not being able to be stronger. It was the hardest and most sad time of my entire life. I missed her terribly. I couldn't stop thinking about how much she would miss me: my little one, my little sunshine. She would miss the morning cuddles, the night tales. At times I got angry at Eli, blaming him for having convinced me to come to Edmonton and leave my girl. Other times I asked myself, without understanding very well, why he assumed such a great responsibility. Did he feel pity for me?

Most days I was grateful for the love, dedication and patience of this wonderful man who took me in his arms, to his house, took care of me and saw what few others saw in me. He could appreciate my virtues despite my being in the darkest moment of my life. Many mornings I woke telling him that I wanted to return, that I could not continue living without my daughter. And he, with wisdom and serenity as always, calmed me down and explained to me, "Marika, life is like a movie. This is just one scene from that movie. And it is the saddest and most difficult scene. Trust that from now on it will be improving. Soon the scene will change, and your daughter will be with you, because it is natural for a child to be with her mother. You have to have some patience, get better, so you can offer your "*ishica*" the best version of yourself.

CHAPTER 4

Life Without my Daughter

March was running along but the days passed slowly. I was learning to drive in the snow and adjusting being far away from my daughter. I talked to her almost daily and that gave me some peace of mind. Little by little I realized that staying in the house was not good for me. I decided to start doing little jobs to distract myself and save money to travel to see her.

I helped a friend bake bread for a few hours. Shortly after, I learned about a lady who had recently had triplets and needed help. I went to the interview to learn that the work was from midnight to six in the morning. The mother needed to rest. I accepted the position. Rochi and her husband were ultra-religious Jews. The triplets were just three weeks old. I had to wash clothes, sterilize bottles and feed the babies when they woke. The first day, when the babies were asleep, and the house was quiet, I realized that helping gave me strength, that my life was beginning to make sense again. If I saved the money earned, I could travel to visit my daughter very soon. According to my calculations, I could be with her in a month. I put in the first load of washing. I put the bottles to boil.

There was a lot of backlogged work to do. The poor mother could not cope.

As I folded delicious baby smelling clothes, I heard one of the triplets crying. I went to the room with a bottle ready and I took the girl in my arms. I snuggled her into my lap and gave her a drink. How many memories came to my mind, how many yearnings. My baby had grown and was so far away!

I did not have the opportunity to dwell much more on my thoughts and memories. I heard the other two babies start crying. I held the first girl with the right hand and two bottles in the left. I tried to put the one I had been feeding in the crib without luck. He started crying and I did not want to wake up the mother. Suddenly, an idea occurred to me. I laid each baby in her basket, rolled up three towels and placed them under each chin to hold the bottles in the correct angle. I was able to give the bottles three at a time.

Meanwhile, I was thinking how I would hold them so that they do their little burps. "Impossible," I reasoned. The most I could do was hold two babies at once. I watched them as they sucked. The youngest was falling asleep during her feeding. I took her in my arms and helped her burp. I laid her in the crib, and she continued to sleep peacefully. Now I was ready. I had both hands free for the other two babies when they finished. "It's not easy," I thought. I had to solve difficult situations, since there were three babies in my charge and I only had two hands. It was a lot of work and for sure a major responsibility.

Rochi woke up the next morning and looked rested. She could not believe that she finally slept a whole night without hearing anything. She thanked me very much.

I arrived home and Eli was waiting to hear about my first day of work. I told him that it was very difficult, almost impossible, since with only two hands, I could not attend three babies. I told him I was going to call Rochi later to tell her that I would not be able to continue. Eli, wise, and knowing me, said, "No problem. She'll find someone who can do the job."

His words echoed in my head, "Can anyone do it? And what about my plans to go see my daughter?" I went to rest and thought about Eli's response. If another person was able to do it, I could do it too. They were not the world's first triplets. After all, Rochi needed help. I saw how thankful she was that morning. I could help her. It was worth the effort. I returned that night and many more after.

Rochi became a sister to me. She taught me about religion without pressuring me or trying to transform me, always with great respect and love. She taught me English and had the patience to correct me and explain when I said something wrong. The babies were a blessing during the months I was away from my daughter. With them, I found a place to give my love and dedication, and I was appreciated. I could hug, sing and pamper. I really gave my best.

For them it was a great effort to pay me for the hours I worked. I voluntarily stayed countless extra hours, because I saw how difficult it was for Rochi to do everything alone. Also, we had a great time. Rochi was a very active woman. We went out for walks with the babies, we chatted, we organized meetings, and met with her friends. We cooked together, went shopping and talked about everything.

The month passed quickly between diapers and bottles and I managed to save the money to travel to see my daughter. On her birthday, April 26, I was in Uruguay to celebrate with her.

It was not the wonderful reunion I had expected. My daughter was angry with me. She did not understand why I had to leave her again, why she could not come with me. How could I explain to a little girl that I wanted to take her with me, but her dad would not allow it?

I was convinced my daughter had to be with me even if I had to live under a bridge. Of course, I wasn't. A mother's love is irreplaceable, but my ex didn't think the same. Since leaving, Flor, lived most of the week with Bea, her father's girlfriend. Bea was great but she was not Flor's mother. My ex only saw his daughter on weekends because he worked in Argentina.

My parents helped them a lot which made me very angry with them. That was not what they had agreed to in front of Eli and me before we left for Canada. I explained to my parents that as long as they continued to help her dad, he would never let her go with me. They enabled him. Ten days later, I returned to Canada weak, sad and discouraged. There seemed no end to this ordeal.

When would the scene Eli predicted show up? When would my daughter get on the plane with me, while her dad peacefully say goodbye to her at the airport? Would that day ever come? At that moment it was hard for me to believe in.

A Heartbreaking Visit

I returned to help Rochi, which gave me a sense of purpose and distracted me from troubling thoughts. Slowly I began to develop a routine. I went to the gym regularly, ate healthy food and worked. - As I write, a powerful memory that brings me to tears comes to mind. I can see myself running on the treadmill closing my eyes and imagining running towards my little girl. It was hard.

On Fridays, after cleaning the house and baking bread, with a nice homey feeling, I would lie down in my room in the sunshine, and I would nap while I waited for Eli. I started to feel happier and more at peace. Eli was an excellent partner and knew how to give me hope.

Say YES, Ask questions later

That July, my parents with my daughter visited us. After a frustrating morning searching for a rental van so we could all travel to the Rockies, we came up with the idea to buy one. It was easier than renting! An hour later, we were driving a brand-new van. We took ownership of the vehicle without a down payment, with the first installment due in ninety days. My dad could not believe how easily everything worked in Canada! We spent a week in the mountains.

My parents were amazed with the generous nature of the country, and its mesmerizing landscapes. But they were most impressed by the order in which things worked and the respect within Canadian society. They loved our modest house, which we had slowly turned into a home with much love and money we were saving.

My daughter was happy. She never left my side even for a moment! We ran, we played, we pampered ourselves, we slept together. I took her to meet the triplets. She adored them; she was a little mommy. She changed them, put them to sleep, they were like dolls for her, and there were three! The relationship with Rochi was almost instantaneous. Love at first sight.

All this joy made the upcoming separation even more difficult than I had imagined. My daughter did not want to go back to Uruguay, and my parents noticed it. They suggested leaving her with me, and they would talk to my ex.

I did not agree. Things had to be done properly. As much as I wished with all my heart that my daughter could stay, I did not want legal problems. He had to sign authorization papers and he had to give her his blessing. He and my daughter had to be at peace with the decision, so she went back to Uruguay with my parents.

The farewell was heartbreaking. Flor cried without stopping and, between cries, pleaded, "Grandma, why do they break my heart?" It was what we had to endure.

She knew her father adored her, and it was difficult for him to let her go. However, he did not see how much more it cost his daughter to be separated from her mother. Upon their return, my parents shared the wonders they had seen, the opportunities ahead, how good our girl was with me, and they suggested that my ex travel to see it with his own eyes. They even offered to pay for the trip.

He was outraged. Who were they to tell him what he should do? Who were they to know what was best for his daughter? And so, out of anger, he decided not to let my parents see their granddaughter for a long time.

Patience, a Quality I Had Not Developed

At the end of October, I traveled to Uruguay again. I stayed until February 13.

Say YES, Ask questions later

I continued with my exercise routine and my healthy diet. I felt at ease and happy to be with my daughter. I took her to school; we went to the beach and spent a lot of time together.

Eli arrived in January and we enjoyed a lot of extended family activities. Eli had owned a restaurant at one time and is a gourmet chef. He was delighted with how fresh the food was, whether it was fruits and vegetables from the market, or the fish and seafood from the port.

The days were advancing quickly, and I was getting very anxious. My ex had not given us an answer as to whether he would let us take Flor to Canada. And so, the day before traveling, on February 12, he called to tell me that if I could find a lawyer to prepare the documents, he would allow her to travel with us. It was not easy to find a lawyer on a Saturday afternoon in February, but the word 'impossible' was not going to interfere with taking my child with me. That same afternoon, with my little daughter jumping in the armchairs of the lawyer's office, we signed the papers without fighting or arguing. We signed everything, just as he wanted.

We packed our suitcases, purchased our tickets and celebrated with the signed papers in our hands. Once again, Eli had been right. After nine months of coming and going and so much suffering, my daughter finally came to stay with us forever.

It had been nine long, hard months, enough to establish a new beginning, but also to experience guilt, sadness, and take on a lot of learning. I learned that in order to take care of her, I had to learn to take care of myself. Patience is a fundamental tool in life and in order to obtain it, it was necessary for me to go through so much suffering. In that time, I also learned not to despair. I learned not to judge other people or their decisions. Who knows the hidden motives and circumstances in each story? I learned to listen to my heart and take charge of my choices, regardless of the opinions or judgments of others. Still today, more than once, I have thought, "I wish I'd *never* had to leave my daughter."

But life is not always what we want. Life *is*. And the only way I could learn that was by staying loyal to my values in the best way I could as I moved forward with what I knew.

CHAPTER 5

All Together in Canada

In the year 2000, who would have imagined that love could exist more than eleven thousand kilometers away? Who would have said that through a cable attached to the wall my mother would find the love of her life? And who would have said that love would start a life in another country?

After six years and curiosity to last at least sixty more, I arrived in Canada with many questions and few expectations. It was February and it was cold. "How can it be cold in February if summer just ended?" I asked Mom.

She explained that in Canada the seasons are inverted, and we were in the middle of winter. How can it be? I thought. There were too many things going on to continue with that question.

A man with a kind face came up and kissed my mom. He said, "Hello! Me 'yamo' Eli, 'muncho' pleasure!"

Yamo? Muncho pleasure? This man did not even know Spanish!

How was I going to live in a house with him, a man who doesn't speak Spanish, and I didn't speak English?

The beginning of my experience in Canada was different.

Mariana Konsolos

There was no ocean, but there was snow. Nobody spoke Spanish and there were no croissants which I loved so much.

Yes, there was a man who loved my mom, but there was no swimming pool in our house.

My mom and Eli spoke to each other in Hebrew. And here I thought English was difficult!

I didn't understand a thing.

When the first day of school arrived, Mom was very nervous. She was worried because I was not going to be able to communicate with anyone. But I wasn't nervous about anything. The day before, she bought me markers to take to school. We went to a place called Costco and I could not believe the things I saw: pens, toys, clothing, food, all in enormous quantities. Nothing like this existed in Uruguay. Mom bought me a box of markers that had more than a hundred colors.

Then I said, "Do not worry, Mom. I don't need to speak English to make friends. I have more than one hundred markers of different colors."

Flor

We arrived in Canada on February 14. I was the happiest person in the world. Now we were all together as a family. My daughter was happy to be with her new big sister Rebecca. She hugged her, kissed her and looked for any way to get her attention.

Say YES, Ask questions later

When we got into the car at the airport to go home, Rebecca put on lipstick. Flor asked her between grimaces and words that I was whispering in her ear in English, if she could also put on the lipstick.

Rebecca replied, "No. I don't share my lipstick with anyone."

"Why not?" asked Flor, surprised

"Because these are personal things," she answered. "You don't want to catch something from others."

We saw the cultural differences from the first day they met. I was worried about how we would build a bridge between them. Time would tell, I thought to myself.

We got organized. I continued working at night with the triplets to pay for my daughter's school fees, until she acquired Canadian citizenship. Eli and I decided on a civil marriage to and then to start the application process for Canadian Citizenship as soon as possible. We were informed the process would take about six months. Flor started classes in April, and her first day of classes was very difficult for me. We chose a bilingual school where children learned English and Hebrew, languages she didn't know at all. When I was leaving, in an attempt to calm me down as a friend would, Flor said in her happy and mischievous little voice, "Don't worry, Mommy, I have a hundred new color markers. Everyone will want to be my friend."

I cried a lot when I was in the parking lot so she couldn't see me. She was so terribly naive! Once again, I felt guilty and self-reproachful. Why did I put her in that situation?

The Edmonton school board informed us that Flor was authorized to attend English as a Second Language (ESL), a special program for children without English experience. She spent the first three months happily absorbing English and Hebrew like a sponge. She was making friends, enjoying the snow, and being with me. After school she loved going to play with the triplets which, of course, was very helpful for Rochi.

On September 11, 2001, the terrible attack on the Twin Towers occurred in New York. All Canadian immigration papers were stopped and the paperwork for thousands of people postponed, including ours. We were informed we would not have citizenship status in time for Flor to continue in school. They advised us to request an extension of our tourist visas, and at the same time, apply for a student visa for Flor. So, we did.

Within a few weeks we received the awaited answer by mail. The extension of my tourist visa had been granted, but Flor's wasn't! The official letter stated that hers was denied because the six-year-old girl had breached the law by attending school in the preceding months in a program that included, in addition to English, another language. Therefore, the

Say YES, Ask questions later

child should leave the country immediately or she would be expelled by the Canadian authorities by force. We couldn't believe it. It couldn't be real. It had to be a mistake.

The phone rang. A call from the school to ask me to pick up Flor immediately. They had been informed by the school board that our girl was not authorized to study. How could I explain to my child these legalities that I did not myself understand? We were disoriented. We didn't know what to do. We called Kim, a very good Canadian friend of Eli's, had her read the letter and tell us if we understood correctly. "Yes," Kim said, "you are going to need a lawyer."

Flor was removed from school that same day. She was crying and didn't understand what was happening. She asked me if she had done something wrong. I tried to explain that no, it was a problem of adults, that we were going to solve it and she would be able to go back to school soon.

In the days that followed we moved like persons possessed. Eli visited his Member of Parliament to explain the situation and ask for help. We spoke with a number of immigration officers over the phone asking for advice and each one offered us a different answer. After speaking with several lawyers, we were more confused than ever. All of them agreed that we should not take Flor out of the country, but we should keep trying to try to find solutions from within Canada.

With my poor English, I called UNICEF out of pure desperation. Why does my daughter not have the right to study if we are paying for it? They responded with total coldness, "Madame, there are more than thirty thousand cases like yours in Canada and unfortunately our hands are tied. Sorry, we cannot help you."

Now I was seeing the other side of the tidy and systematic Canadian government. It was a heartless system which didn't consider exceptions. There was no one to talk to. In my eyes all this was absurd. But the system was prepared exactly for that: not to be able to speak or explain anything to a human being in person, to avoid corruption, I guess.

Someone recommended the best immigration lawyer. It cost us a fortune, at least for us at the time, nevertheless we dug into our savings to hire her. She wrote a letter explaining the whole situation, asking for an extension of the girl's tourist visa, detailing we were in the process of applying for permanent residency in Canada, but proceedings were delayed by the September 11 events. What she really did was to buy time, in the hope that our papers would be issued in that period. We hired a private tutor to avoid Flor falling behind in school. The rest of each day we spent together.

It was a difficult time for me, but I learned how to occupy our hours doing incredible crafts: models of small cities with school and supermarket, dolls in the

Say YES, Ask questions later

squares and blue lakes. We painted with watercolors, made boxes with ice cream sticks, and made dolls with torn stockings. We became expert bakers of braided bread and funky and delicious cookies. We went for swimming lessons and tried to relax.

Rochi, the mom of the triplets, was a kindergarten teacher in a small semi-private school. She invited us to her classroom often. It was quite an experience to watch her teach her students. The children adored her, and I understood why. She was passionate and her classes were full of profound teachings Flor and I too were enriched by lessons that stayed with us forever. One of the things I remember most of those days is how my daughter's eyes filled with joy every time we were invited to Rochi's classroom. Flor was missing out on the opportunity to spend time playing with other children.

As time passed, we started to get impatient as we waited for a response through our lawyer. Soon we learned that calling her was only costing us money, not getting us ahead. We were worried. The date of our wedding in Uruguay was approaching and the plane tickets were already bought. Our lawyer and several immigration officials advised us not to leave the country with Flor under any circumstances because none of them could guarantee that she would be allowed to re-enter Canada.

What would we do if the papers did not arrive before our trip? Would we cancel the trip to Uruguay and the wedding? Would we go anyway and take all the risks? What if they really didn't let her back into Canada? Where would we go?

I wasn't ready to go back to Uruguay to stay! I started looking for alternatives. I inquired about Miami, Costa Rica, even Panama. Every day I waited in the living room as the postman passed our door. I began to feel anxiety, and slowly the depression returned.

Eli was very worried. I was rapidly losing hope and, added to the cold weather, I was rarely leaving the house. From Argentina, Flor's father asked, "How could it be the girl wasn't going to school?"

I was under a lot of pressure and Eli noticed that I was not handling it very well. On a November afternoon he returned from work. I welcomed him with the same anxiety and the same old question, "What are we going to do? Time is running out."

Eli hugged me, looked into my eyes and said, "Marika, our marriage is not postponed. We are going to be together, no matter where. We will follow our plans. What happens with the procedures does not depend on us. We will solve it when the situation arises. Everything has a solution." His words were the best medicine for me. Again, I felt calm and safe. Eli made decisions when I couldn't and that allowed me to fall more in love with him every day.

Say YES, Ask questions later

Our Big, Fat Jewish Wedding

When Rebecca got into the car after her Wednesday dance class, she happily announced that she was allowed to come with us to Uruguay for our wedding. It was the first time she would visit Uruguay and knowing she was going to be part of our special day made us more excited than we already were. That night, while the four of us were having dinner, chatting animatedly about our upcoming trip to Punta del Este, she took out a list, handed it to Eli and said, "I can go if I can abide by what's on the list." Her father put it in his pocket and announced he would read it later. I was dying of curiosity, since Rebecca was not a demanding girl at all.

After dinner, when we went to bed, Eli took out the list. After reading it was handed to me. The list read: don't drink tap water, go to bed by nine o'clock at night, sleep at least twelve hours a day, don't go to the beach more than three hours between such and such hours. The list went on and on. I couldn't believe it! Life in Punta del Este was completely different from Canada. Going to the beach was the activity of choice. We were used to spending full days at the beach bathing and having lunch with friends! We never went to sleep before two in the morning as the mornings started late. And, to make things worse, we did drink tap water.

"We cannot take her with us," I said to Eli sadly.

He laughed. "When we are there, she will want to do what we all do, and I know how much she will enjoy it. The only problem is she doesn't know where she's going, so she's afraid. She thinks she's going to the middle of the jungle. She'll be surprised you will see. Trust me, you don't need to worry. She will be fine." I loved that fresh and positive outlook from Eli. He never allowed problems to develop or steal our attention before their time.

Finally, the preparations for the wedding began. Every day we received news from different people who were travelling for the wedding. Rebecca and Flor began to practice a ballet piece to perform. Eli's mother and older sister bought tickets to come from Israel. I was especially happy my grandmother Sara, almost one hundred years old, would be with us at such an important moment in my life. My beloved friend Lea, the singer, would travel from London, where she was studying music. She was going to perform at our party with her *a cappella* group singing in Ladino to honour my mother-in- law-, the old Spanish of the Sephardic Jews who were expelled from Spain five hundred years ago.

Dubon, my travel companion during my teen years, would be the organist at the religious ceremony. Andrea, my Chilean friend, Denise and Sandra, from Buenos Aires, Tammy, my sister of the heart, would all be at the wedding. And of course, my family.

Say YES, Ask questions later

It was very special for Eli and me, as it would be our first wedding following the sacred Jewish ritual for both of us.

My friend from Edmonton, Miky, loaned me her wedding dress. Rochi gave Eli a *kippah* for the religious ceremony, blessed by a respected rabbi from New York.

Together with Flor, with the best of craftsmanship and full of love, we created the invitation cards for our wedding. They were simply beautiful: white, with a yellow daisy on the cover. I loved them!

I was living a dream! As the date for our trip got closer, the lawyer sent a letter to the immigration office, explaining the particulars of the situation. She feared if the documents would arrive in our absence, the process could be canceled, and we would find ourselves at square one.

I waited at the window, wishing the postman would deliver the so famous documents that would prevent us from stressing out on our way back to Canada. But they never arrived.

*****

Our wedding was intimate, elegant and full of emotion. The backyard at my parents' home was more beautiful than ever. The intense green grass contrasted with the white chairs that lined up next to a flower bed. Beside it was the awning, or *jupa* where the religious ceremony would take place.

Under a large white tent, dinner would be served to our guests. Everything was elegantly set. Slender centerpieces with fresh flowers in pastels and very white tablecloths were ready to entertain our international crowd.

That day I was reflecting about the path we had traveled, the shared challenges and the unconditional love that this wonderful man gave me day after day for the past year. This was the man that I could only dream might exist and who had chosen me to travel life's path with forever. I couldn't prevent my tears.

I believe what made me feel extra emotional was the fact we were going to get married according to the religion of our ancestors. It gave our wedding a special mysticism.

Our wedding was not all traditional, though. Our daughters were present to celebrate with us!

The ceremony began when we arrived at the *jupa* accompanied by our parents, brothers and daughters. The rabbi blessed us and proceeded to perform the traditional rite.

Eli looked at me enraptured and my heart beat uncontrollably. Before finishing the ceremony, the rabbi addressed us. With the wisdom of the one who knows enamored souls, he offered his wise words, "God gave us two eyes. An eye to see the good things of our partner and the other eye to look at ourselves and see the things we can improve."

Now, seventeen years have passed since that night and I can still remember every detail as if I was experiencing it for the first time. I smell the flowers and taste the cakes. I laugh with the witty speech of my brother, where he thanked Bill Gates for technology that made meeting Eli possible. I see our daughters, dancing with a blue scarf that simulated the ocean, the deep voice of Lea resounds in my ears singing old songs in Ladino that moved my mother-in-law and my sister-in-law to tears. I see our friend Aliza entering absolutely by surprise, with that wonderful costume embroidered in a thousand colors. She carried a golden candelabra with six candles lit over her head and so delighted us with a spectacular belly dance that left all the guests speechless. And my Rochi, who couldn't accept not being there with us, smuggled life size photos of my adored triplets into my suitcase.

Those who were present reminded us how much love was felt and lived on the night of our wedding. Our love came out through our pores and we couldn't and didn't want to hide it.

CHAPTER 6

My First Work Steps

As expected, our longed-for papers arrived while we were in Uruguay celebrating our marriage.

Rochi went to the immigration office with the letter and they told her there were no problems; as soon as we arrived home from our trip, we should contact them, and everything would be fine. She sent us a copy of the letter that gave us legal residence in Canada. Finally, Flor would be able to go to school. We returned very happy. Now everything would start to be normal. As my mom says, "When in movement, melons settle in the cart." We were the melons and our life was like the cart moving us nicely along as we settled in.

When we arrived at the airport, we showed the letter and received a warm welcome. Months of anguish fell behind us. We were now legal residents and entitled to all the rights available to any Canadian.

Flor returned to school happy to find herself far ahead of her class thanks to the private lessons she had taken. This gave her a strong sense of security. That same year she started taking ballet and music lessons, and she practiced both of them for many years.

Say YES, Ask questions later

I attended English lessons as part of a program that the Canadian government offered at no cost to its new residents to ease their integration. I entered Norquest College and was fortunate to meet an exceptional woman there, Elaine. She was much more than an English teacher; she was a life mentor. She taught us important everyday things and introduced us to Canadian culture and customs in a very simple and practical way. The classes were always fun and interesting.

After finishing my second semester, I saw Elaine while having a break and told her, "I am on my way to the office to sign up for the next semester.

"Don't waste your time, I will not accept you," she said seriously.

"Why?" I asked, concerned.

"You are ready to go out into the real world." she answered. She continued, "Here, among other immigrants, you feel very comfortable because you are at the top of the class. It is time for you to go out and immerse yourself in Canadian culture, where you'll feel uncomfortable, but you'll learn many new things. Your vocabulary will expand only with use in everyday life."

I thought about what she told me, and I felt she was right. The following week I enrolled in a job interview workshop. There I learned how to create my *curriculum vitae* the Canadian way. I presented it to dozens of businesses. I would be called for interviews, which got me excited, but then they would ask if I had Canadian experience. Since my answer was *no*, they would not hire me.

One afternoon I went to Pier One to look for some cushions I needed for our living room. By the door I spotted a "hiring now" sign. I asked to speak with the manager and as I handed her my CV, she asked me if I was willing to have an interview at that moment. "Of course!" I replied. She interviewed me for a long hour and finally told me she would call me within the week. I loved that store and desperately wanted to work there. The days passed, and the phone call never came. I decided to call Elaine, the ESL teacher from NorQuest, to ask her opinion. She suggested I call the store and insist on speaking with the person who had interviewed me. Maybe she was busy, maybe she had simply forgotten. I followed Elaine's advice. The person who answered the phone told me that the manager had not decided yet but reassured me that in a couple of days she would call me. Again, I waited and again nothing. Three days later I drove to the store. When the manager saw me entering, she smiled. She invited me to her office and offered me the job that I so longed for.

The woman explained to me I would have only a few training hours at first. Additional hours would be added as long as they could evaluate my progress. I accepted happily. My salary was small, but I decided to consider it as my starting point to demonstrate my capability and finally be able launch my retail career in Canada. I was very grateful for the opportunity and when I was about to leave, she pointed out to me, "I'm hiring you because I appreciate your insistence and your desire to work. I'm not so sure if it's going to be a good fit. Time will tell."

That afternoon I called Elaine to share the news. "I am happy for you but more than that, I am very proud of you."

I must admit the first days were hard. It was not easy to understand the vocabulary used by my co-workers and clients. They used their own jargon, and terminology very specific to the home decoration field. I learned names of new colors that I had never heard in my life, what to call the different kinds of glasses, internal names they used to identify dish collections and thousands of other pieces of small information.

There were days when I felt like an idiot, and hardly understood a few words in a full conversation.

Soon I learned the Mariana who existed in Uruguay was not the same person I became in Canada. My English was basic, my vocabulary limited, and my strong accent sometimes made it hard for people to understand me. I felt like they saw me as an uneducated person or someone with an intellectual disability. I was struggling with communication and it was taking a toll on my self-esteem.

Mariana Konsolos

Elaine gave me valuable advice throughout the years. She suggested greeting customers including comments on the weather in Uruguay. That way they would know I wasn't native Canadian as they assumed based on my blonde hair and light eyes. It proved to be an excellent technique. "Good day! How are you doing today? I am very cold. In Uruguay, where I come from, there is no snow," I would say as the customers entered the store, it was like magic! Customers became extra kind and interested to learn about Uruguay and how I ended up in Canada. They spoke to me slowly and had extra patience when I did not understand what they needed.

I had fun serving all kinds of people and I didn't get tired of showing them all the available options. Nobody left the store empty handed. Slowly I learned some repeat customer's names and my good memory helped me remember what they bought in their previous visits and the purpose of their purchase. They flipped when I asked, "Did your friend like the blue vase that you bought her?" Customers truly appreciated the personalized customer service I offered them. I started to find solutions to small problems I encountered. A When someone wanted us to hold an item for them, I had a hard time spelling their name in English. I decided to ask the clients themselves to write down their name and phone number to avoid misspellings. Again, it worked wonders. People were always willing to help when asked.

The company was happy with me and were rewarding me with every shift I requested. I felt I was growing and moving in the right direction. Elaine's voice came to my mind often, "Think as if this job were University. You are learning the necessary skills needed to be the successful entrepreneur you were in Uruguay, but for the Canadian market using the Canadian systems." And she always finished the sentence by adding, "Do you realize they are teaching you and they pay you over and above that!" Her wisdom was underrated. I saw each day of work as an opportunity to grow and improve myself.

Family life, on the other hand, was going smoother. Our finances were tight, but our happiness was abundant.

The Phone

In Uruguay, the telephone was one of my favorite tools. I used it to speak with friends for hours, or to close out real estate transactions with my clients from abroad. But in Canada, it was one of the things I was most afraid of. I hated answering the phone because I didn't understand what people were saying to me. Face to face everything was easier. I would use my hands, make gestures and somehow always manage to make myself understood. By phone it was entirely different. If I did not understand, I did not understand, period. I could repeat the same phrase ten times and still not reach an understanding. This frustrated me a lot.

One afternoon at work, I heard the phone ring. Before this particular day, I somehow managed to ignore it. There was always someone at the counter who liked to answer the phone, but that day it rang where my manager and I were standing. She gestured to me to answer it. I did it as I had been taught, "Good morning, Mariana speaking. How can I help you?"

"Do you have a red [...] in stock?" asked the lady calling. I could not decipher what item she was looking for in red.

So, I tried again, "What are you looking for?"

She repeated over and over and all I understood was she was looking for something red. When the lady realized that I did not understand, she raised her voice and said boldly, "Why do you answer the phone if you do not speak fluent English? Pass me immediately to someone who understands me."

I spoke to the manager and cried as I explained what happened. After attending to the client, my manager called me into her office and told me that she could not believe I still did not know how to answer the phone. It was unacceptable, and she asked me what I thought should be done about it. I felt humiliated and very diminished. The Mariana who managed millionaire businesses and was able to

Say YES, Ask questions later

engage in interesting philosophical and political conversation in Uruguay, now could not, in this Canadian setting, understand a most basic conversation.

I asked to leave early and went home crying. I was convinced that the best thing would be to give up that job and dedicate myself to taking care of children or doing things where I didn't need to speak much.

In the evening I called Elaine. I told her all the details of what happened to me and how badly I felt not only because of the client's attitude, but also because of the manager's harsh words. I told her I intended to resign. She listened to me carefully and asked me a few questions, trying to get as much information as possible, when, suddenly, she started to laugh. I didn't understand what was funny about the story I told her. "Does me feeling like an idiot make you want to laugh?" I asked in disbelief.

With a firm voice she shook me, "Mariana, today is the best day of your life. Today, for the first time, you know what you don't know. You do not know how to answer the phone! You can't live in any country without knowing how to answer the phone! How will you make doctor's appointments for your child? How are you going to call a mechanic if your car breaks down? How are you going to negotiate with a provider if you don't know how to talk on the phone? In order to be the complete Mariana, you have to leave your comfort zone and learn what you don't know. "YOU DON'T KNOW HOW TO ANSWER THE PHONE!" Then she repeated slowly, and in a very loud voice, "Giving up isn't going to solve your problem. It will just make it worse and worse. Every day you will be more afraid of answering the phone. From now on, when the phone rings in the store, you have to run to answer the phone. As she was making her point clearer, she exclaimed as loud as she could, "Furthermore, you should be racing to pick up the darn phone every time it rings in the store!" Going back to her gentle tone she continued, "The more times you answer the phone, the more you will experience less fear. You will understand a little more each day. In time, clients will get used to your accent and you'll recognize more words every day. It doesn't matter if they shout at you, if they speak harshly to you. You have to remember that your only goal is to learn to answer the phone!"

What a lesson my dearest Elaine gave me! How many 'telephones' do we have in front of us in our daily life, and, instead of running to take care of them, we flee in the opposite direction trying to avoid fear of failing or being rejected.

"From now on," I thought, "every time something scares me, I'm going to run towards that something. Fear will be the signal to announce to me I am faced with something unknown to me or something new to

First Visit of my Inspiring Muse

Ideas were coming to me. Customers were noticing and asking about the fashion accessories I wore. They wanted to know where I got them from and asked me for ideas about how they could use their own. Accessories have always been important to me. I like to be well dressed! I knew how to combine things well with a certain grace that people liked. I told Eli what was happening, but he didn't give it much importance. I decided to buy costume jewelry to see what reactions people would have. After asking my manager for permission, I arranged a display in the employee's shared dining room at the store. That day, much to my surprise, I sold almost half of the accessories. I started paying special attention to what people liked most so I could focus my acquisitions toward those same designs. In less than a week I had sold almost everything.

Soon afterward, Flor was participating in a ballet competition and Eli and I went to see her. When we arrived at the theater, I noticed a lady who kept looking at me. Eli asked me if I knew her, but I did not recognize her. The lady came up to us and kindly said, "Excuse me for bothering you, but I was looking at your scarf. It is absolutely exquisite; I've never seen anything like it. Could I ask you where you bought it?"

I blushed and said shyly, "It's from Uruguay in South America."

She seemed bothered by my answer but continued, "I have a suit that I'm going to use for a gala and that scarf is just the color and texture I was looking for. Do you know if I can find it somewhere in Edmonton?"

I replied, "Actually, I have been looking for it myself because a friend of mine also liked it a lot, but unfortunately I have not been able to find it anywhere."

The lady remained pensive for a moment, then asked fast almost as she was trying to hide her embarrassment, "Would you sell it to me? I will pay you 80 dollars cash!"

I looked at Eli and asked him quickly in Hebrew, "Is this normal in Canada?"

"It has never happened to me." He replied while laughing.

I looked at the woman and quickly calculated. Wow, 80 dollars was three days of work in the store. "Yes, I will sell it to you." I removed it from around my neck and handed it to the lady as a trophy. She paid me and left. Eli couldn't believe what he had just seen and heard. He was astonished by what he just witnessed. I really sold a scarf off my neck for 80 dollars. It is true that it was very original and unique. It was silk with wools of irregularly interlaced colors. But it was hard to believe that someone was willing to pay 80 dollars for a used scarf. For us, 80 dollars was a small fortune!

The Graduation

One morning at the store, while helping a client choose carpets, I noticed the manager watching me while she was talking with another lady. That afternoon, she called me into her office. When employees were called to the office it was usually bad news and very rarely for something good. The other lady I spotted earlier in the store was in the office with my manager.

"Mariana, this is Laura, the Regional Manager of the company. Today she is visiting from Toronto." She continued, "Laura, this is Mariana, one of our best sales associates."

I shook hands with Laura and was invited to sit down. They explained to me that the company was in the process of expansion and they would open more stores in the city. Our manager would be responsible for the new project, and so my current store would need a new manager.

I couldn't believe what was about to happen. After two years, they were going to offer me the manager role of the store. They spoke about expectations, shared salary and benefits information, and other interesting details. Laura then said, "We think that you are the ideal candidate for the position, and we wanted to ask you what you think."

I thought it was unreal what I had just heard. I was silent and thoughtful. I got up, went to the desk and humbly told them, "I hope you know how much this means to me and I thank you infinitely for this opportunity." I paused and then continued, "If you think I can manage this business, it means I am ready to manage my own business. A thousand thanks for everything, but not only will I not accept your offer, but, at this very moment, I renounce my current position. It's time to open my own company!"

The two women looked at each other in stupor. "Are you sure?" Laura asked me.

"More sure than I have ever been." I replied confidently.

They wished me luck and told me if I changed my mind, the doors would remain open for me. I gave them each a hug and I left feeling happy.

Once in the car I called Eli. "My love, I need to tell you. They offered me the store manager position ... Thanks ... thanks ... but no, I didn't accept it! What's more, I just quit. No, my love, I'm not crazy. I'm saner than ever. Stay calm. I will create my own benefits and I will work for myself. I feel as if today was my graduation from University. We have to go out to celebrate. OKAY. I'm picking up Flor and I will see you with Rebecca at eight in the Chinese restaurant. I love you! Yes, everything will be fine. Trust me!"

My Daughter Became My Teacher

The days and weeks passed, and I couldn't stop thinking about the scarf I sold at Flor's ballet competition.

"I have to find those scarves! I searched online and nothing. I did not find any that were even close to the mine," I commented one night at dinner.

Flor was listening to our conversation when suddenly she said, "Ma, why don't you make them?"

"Because I don't even know how to sew on a button," I answered without paying too much attention.

"I can teach you," she argued.

"And how do you know how to sew?" I questioned her, surprised.

"Well, when I finish ballet class and I am waiting for you to get me, I observe the ladies who sew dresses. Sometimes I ask them how to make hems or more difficult things and they explain it to me. They even let me sew!"

Eli and I looked at each other. How many more things did this girl know we were not aware of?

"If you buy a sewing machine, I'll show you," Flor told me. Immediately after dinner, we hurried to Walmart to buy a sewing machine.

We bought the cheapest and simplest they had. We bought yarns, wool and pieces of fabric to practice, and came home elated.

As the expert, Flor threaded the needle and explained that first it needed to go here, then there, that the fabric was supposed to go like this ... and she stepped on the pedal and started sewing. We stayed up until midnight trying different things. She showed me how to make hems, how to finish the edges with the different stitches and points I could use. I was speechless. Slowly, after endless hours of practice, I managed to make my first scarves.

They were not identical to the one I sold, but they looked similar. I bought a cute little trunk, bought odds and ends of cheap fabrics and wool on sale of different colors and textures.

A friend suggested that I sell my scarves at the university, where a small fee would allow me to set a table in the canteen. I called and booked it that same week. I must say the display of my scarves was very attractive. The dark brown chest looked old, its lid half-opened and the colored fabrics and wools of varied textures that poked out gave an exotic touch.

The scarves cascaded out from the trunk and showed their wool loops stitched with metallic threads on the semitransparent fabrics.

Many who passed stopped to look and touch. "How much are you selling them for? Shamefully I answered, "Twenty." I explained they could also choose the fabric and wool of their choice from the trunk and I would sew them a scarf combining the

Say YES, Ask questions later

elements of their choice if they wanted. This would be their custom made and original scarf.

"You make them?" was always the next question.

"Yes," I replied proudly, and that was *the* moment.

People were enlightened and inspired and asked, "Can you make it for me tomorrow? I can leave you a deposit."

"No need," I said. "Tomorrow, when I have it ready, you can pay for it." Generally, clients returned the next day to look for their scarves. If they did not return, I did not worry. Sooner or later they all sold to someone. Customers started to recommend me to their friends. When Christmas arrived, there was a big explosion and orders were getting bigger. They asked me for three, five, ten, fifteen pieces. People saw my handmade scarves as a unique and original gift at a very reasonable price. They were ideal for friends, colleagues and family.

The orders didn't stop and to fulfill them all, I was sewing nonstop until the wee hours. It was a sacrifice, but I really loved what I was doing! With practice I managed to sew a complete scarf in thirty minutes. When one scarf was finished, I would look at it with pride and think, "Who would have imagined that I could sew thanks to my daughter!" We never know when something we learn will come handy in the course of our life. Everything we learn goes into our knowledge archive and is available for us to use when needed.

Mariana Konsolos

Eli used to joke that during that time he forgot how my face looked. When he got home, he would find me with my back bent over the sewing machine with its unbearable tu-tu-tu-tu-tu-tu-tu clattering throughout the night. That Christmas I sewed more than four hundred scarves! I was exhausted but very proud of myself. I generated many dollars for the family in just over two hundred hours of work. "It's not bad," I told myself. At night I fell asleep thinking about what I would need to do to sew twice as many scarves for the following Christmas.

CHAPTER 7

Growth

My back hurt a lot after spending so many hours at the sewing machine. I had less time and even less desire to do housework. I must confess that I never liked it before, so, since there was no budget for a cleaner, I decided to find another way to create the income for that purpose. I started ironing three nights a week which provided enough money to hire a housekeeper to wash clothes and clean our house once a week. I was much happier and less stressed. I didn't mind ironing because usually, the employer stayed chatting with me while I ironed. That's how I met new people and made new friends.

"Everything has a solution, but it implies being willing to make the necessary sacrifices," said Eli.

I still had some costume jewelry from Argentina and decided to look for places where I could sell it. As a family we started thinking about a name for my new business. Rebecca agreed that I could use her photo on the business cards. In honor of Flor we called the company Princess Florence, because she was always my princess! It was a way to have them both with me every day.

My friend Neora worked in a nursing home and told me that other vendors were permitted there. I called the next day and managed to coordinate a date to offer my products. It was a simple place, with a central courtyard filled with trees and plants. There I set up with my trunk and my Argentinian treasures. The residents bought very little. They were more interested to find someone to chat with.

My English was improving due to the long conversations I was having with the residents. I loved listening to them, because they taught me so much about Canada and their stories were inspiring. There were stories of immigrants, of great sacrifices and courageous lives. They made me think of my grandmothers ... I had never made time to sit with them and ask the details of when they arrived in Uruguay. My grandma Sara was still alive, and I hardly knew her. I promised myself to visit her and start a relationship when I returned to Uruguay.

"How much do the rings cost?" asked one of the nurses.

"Oh, 10 dollars," I said.

"That's all? Would you put it aside for me until my break in half an hour, so I can bring you the money?"

"Of course!" I replied.

"I will tell my coworkers. They don't know you're here and they're going to love what you have. Also, the prices are very reasonable. Thank you!"

I was happy. The hours passed quietly between talks and sales. They allowed me to come once a month, so I searched for more seniors' residences to fill my calendar.

Say YES, Ask questions later

One of the things I loved the most was, after a month when I returned to the residence, two or three of the resident friends I had met the month before would be waiting anxiously at the front door. These ladies were between eighty and ninety-five years old, and when I arrived loaded up with boxes, they would always offer to help. They were so kind!

Since most of them walked with the help of a walker, I told them very seriously, "Do you know what I really need? A coffee and some cookies." Then they would walk as fast as their legs would allow and they would make me coffee and bring me the cookies they started to keep for me from their breakfast. It was an act of love that touched me deeply each time it happened. They felt useful; they had a reason to get up that morning.

There were lonely souls eager to do something valuable for someone. They had a lot to give and they had no one to give it to. It was very sad to watch, and sadder when I started losing those old friends. It affected me a lot. I had learned so much from them. I felt they left without having shared enough experiences with me and the rest of the world. Each was a unique piece of art carved by the years and the blows of their long lives.

At first the sales were small, but as the weeks and months went by, I managed to book more nursing homes where I could set up my little booth. The nurses suggested I also try to sell at hospitals as they had more traffic. After calling five hospitals, I was allowed to set up at one.

Between sewing scarves and closing sales, I was busy and managed to generate more profits than the salary I had in the home decor store. I no longer needed to iron for others in order to be able to pay the cleaning lady. My work life was adjusting so I did not take away from family time. I would finish selling scarves around three o'clock in the afternoon, after which I would go looking for Flor and sometimes Rebecca when she was staying with us. After picking them up from school, I would take them to their piano or ballet lessons. Eli enjoyed buying groceries and cooking, so he happily took care of those tasks. It was really nice to get home and have dinner ready. Eli's cooking was healthy and also delicious.

Somehow, I heard there was an upcoming gift and fashion trade show for wholesalers in Edmonton and I decided to attend. While I was touring the show, I was struck by a collection of very unique silver jewelry. The name of the company was written in Hebrew. I went to look more closely at the collection and a very kind lady introduced herself, "Good afternoon! Do you have a business?" Immediately I could recognize within her English the use of the strong "r" and the intense "j".

"No, I don't have a business," I replied, and added, "But I do speak Hebrew."

Say YES, Ask questions later

We had a very nice conversation sharing the details of our respective life stories. After a while, she asked me if I would be interested in selling their products. I replied that I loved the line, but that silver was expensive, and I was just beginning, and I didn't have the money to invest. She replied without hesitation, "If you come at the end of the day, I will leave you some products on consignment. You will receive a percentage of what you sell. How about that? What do you think?"

I didn't expect such an offer, but instinctively I said, "YES!" As I walked away from the booth, I called Eli to tell him about the offer. "What risk could there be? I would have new products without investing my own money." He gave me the green light to take the offer. There was really nothing to lose.

When it was closing time at the fair, Tmima was waiting for me with a big box of jewelry. She wrote out an invoice with a total cost price of ten thousand dollars. As I saw the number, my eyes opened wide. She noticed the surprise on my face and playfully asked me, "Do you know what my name, Tmima means, in Hebrew?"

I said yes, "Naive."

She laughed and added, "I am naive, but not stupid. I know how to recognize good people. You know how to sell, and you are an honest person."

That same night we invited Tmima and Adi, her husband for dinner at our house. Eli prepared a real feast for us. Needless to say, to this day we are very good friends, despite the fact we live in different countries, and over the years we stopped buying their products. They believed in me and gave me a big opportunity that I have never failed to be thankful for.

Another Great Mentor

One afternoon I went to an open ballet class to watch Flor dance. I sat in a corner of the room, when Tema soon entered. Her presence inspired respect. Short white hair and marked facial features. She dressed soberly and didn't wear makeup. She took a seat next to me.

"I am Tema, Oriana's mother," she said in a sweet voice that I could not have predicted.

"Flor told me a lot about your daughter," I replied. I introduced myself feeling intimidated. After reviewing a question in my head a few times so as not to make grammatical mistakes, I dared to ask her, "Why did you call your daughter Oriana?"

"For an Italian writer, Oriana Fallaci. Do you know her?"

"Yes, she's one of my favorites. Not many people know about her. At least not in Uruguay." (I was using Elaine's trick mentioning Uruguay to make clear I wasn't a native speaker). We started talking

Say YES, Ask questions later

about the writer's books, about Uruguay and the reasons that brought me to Canada. Tema told me about her family, her travels and experiences in different countries they visited in sabbatical years.

Later that week Flor was invited to a playdate at Oriana's house. Eli drove me to pick her up. As we arrived, I got out of the car to ring the bell. Tema's husband opened the door. I was surprised when I first saw him. I knew he was an engineering professor, but he was not what I expected. He was super friendly, jovial, with an ultramodern haircut, and wearing very tight and colorful clothes. He greeted me in a way that surprised me., "Hello! Nice to meet you! You must be Flor's mom." He wouldn't wait for my answer. Instead he proceeded to hug me and kiss me on both cheeks. I could not believe it! I had never experienced this in Canada where people do not greet strangers with kisses or hugs. He continued, "Come in, come in! I have peach pie fresh from the oven."

I was in shock. During my years in Canada, nobody had ever invited me for coffee or pie whenever I picked up my daughter from playdates. It was snowy and cold that day, I wanted badly to say YES, but I needed to ask Eli, therefore I responded, "My husband is in the car. Let me see if we have commitments this afternoon."

I went back to the car to tell Eli about the invitation, thinking, "He's not going to accept, he's shy. What a pity! I'd love to get to know these people better."

But he didn't give me time. He followed me and, approaching Eli, opened the car door and said, "Hello. Come, come down and try the delicious pie that I just baked. I also have an exotic tea that I brought from France, which I'm sure you'll love."

Eli couldn't say no. After all, he was talking about food, one of Eli's favorite topics.

It was really amazing! This was the first time I experienced such spontaneity in Canada! The affinity was obvious. We really enjoyed our diversities. They were conservative l academics. We, the unpredictable entrepreneurs. Their life was rational and structured, while ours was navigated in pursuit of opportunities presented to us.

Perhaps the attraction of these polar opposites created this close relationship with Tema and her husband, a relationship that has lasted over the years. Tema and I share many interests such as same aged daughters, a fascination with entrepreneurship, creating new things in the community, but, above all, we share the same values: loyalty, honesty, trust and sincere desire to see our neighbor succeed. Tema has accompanied me in every instance of my growth, both work and personal during the entire time I've known her. From that moment we met she has been at my side ready to give me intelligent and honest advice.

Say YES, Ask questions later

New Opportunities on the Horizon

Home Parties

Holly, an accounting manager in a very warm and welcoming nursing home in the eastern part of the city, approached me one day while I was selling. She proposed, "Mariana, I spoke to my friends about you and your fashion accessories. They are interested in meeting you and seeing your collection. Would you like to have a party at my house?"

Innocently, I looked at her and asked, "YES, but...what is a party?"

She smiled, "Have you heard about Tupperware parties? A company who does home gatherings where they include product presentations, explain the benefits and women buy from them?"

I looked at her in horror but managed to respond, "But I don't want to speak or explain anything in front of many women. My English is not good enough!"

She smiled again, amused by my honesty. Then she told me, "Don't worry. Don't explain anything. Just bring your things and if people ask, you will answer as you do here. How about that?"

"That I can do!" I agreed.

I came home happy and told Eli, "What a good idea this 'party thing' will be!"

The party at Holly's was an incredible experience. I went early, prepared my table and made a very elegant and elaborate display. Shawls were draped on the table, with copper vases from Israel, where the jewelry came from, and picture frames that served as displays for the silver necklaces were arranged. I chose aromatic candles to add a sophisticated fragrance complementing the sensorial experience, transporting the clients to exotic lands.

Holly and Des, her daughter, made me feel at home. They worried about me, explaining what I didn't understand. They showed my treasures as if they were theirs. Our guests went crazy. They fought over accessories. I didn't have to sell anything; my pieces sold themselves!

Everyone was more interested in hearing my story, where I came from, the love story with Eli than having me talk about the jewellery I brought. I was sharing one of my stories when my phone rang. I excused myself to answer a call from my mom. When I started speaking in Spanish, the women looked at me enraptured. I heard them say, "What a divine language, look what a beautiful accent!" I spoke quickly with my mom and explained I was busy. When I hung up, I remembered the wise words of Elaine, my English teacher. Every time I asked her to correct my accent, she counselled me, "If you lose your accent, you stop being Mariana. Don't try to be the same as everyone else, because you are not! You are different. Your accent makes you unique and exotic. Feel proud of who you are!"

Say YES, Ask questions later

That night I understood exactly what Elaine wanted to tell me. I was different, and people were attracted to that. I didn't need to be ashamed of my accent. My accent meant a different culture and the ability to speak another language. My weeks were filling up with more and more activities. I sold at the university, some nursing homes, one hospital and did home-parties in the evenings. Revenues were increasing. I took a leap and decided to incorporate handbags. I ordered eight of them, and they were an incredible success. Those eight later became eighty which sold like hotcakes. Everywhere I went I met a lot of new people, I chatted with many of them, and I made sure to hand out a business card to anyone who wanted one so we could stay in touch.

Conferences

One day, I received a call from a lady I met during one of her visits to her mother in a nursing home. She was in charge of a conference her workplace was organizing for International Women's Day and she thought having my fashion accessories would be a nice treat for the ladies. I loved the idea. I thanked her for thinking of me. I wrote the date, time, address and her personal phone number. I called Eli to share the news. As the professional taxi driver, he was, he knew every street and building of the city. As I read the address back to him, he thought for a second and said, "What? Do you know where you're going?"

"Yes, to a conference for International Women's Day".

"The lady works in the women's prison! Are you going to sell there?" he said.

"Yes, I will. I'm not scared," I replied. I found it an interesting experience, since I had never before entered a prison. The prisoners helped me load the boxes and asked for permission to buy some of my products. The conference was very interesting, there were several speakers, and everything was new to me. That afternoon I sold more than 2,000 dollars in just a few hours!

Exploring New Cities in the Province

Another day I received a call from a hospital. I jumped for joy. I coordinated all the details and, as always, I called Eli. He laughed again, "Do you know where that hospital is? It's in Fort McMurray! Five hours driving from here. Cancel it. It's way too far."

"No way! I said YES, I gave my word, I will go!" I answered confidently.

That was my motto—first say 'YES', ask questions later." If I said "yes," I would go no matter what. My word was worth more than any contract. There was no event, fair or hospital that I found too small or big, too distant or hard to find, that I couldn't attend. I saw each one as an opportunity to discover new markets, new ideas or new contacts. Each place was totally different, and for me all were possibilities. I realized that this slightly naive touch offered me advantages, since I had no prejudices or limiting beliefs about them. I had the grit and was willing to make all the necessary sacrifices to make my business successful. I realized it was also a great opportunity to immerse myself in the culture and discover the geography of the country.

What is a Consultant?

The phone rang. I picked it up.

"Good morning, Princess Florence, how can I help you?"

"Hi, very nice to meet you. My name is Pam. I saw you the other day at the hospital. I loved your products. I would like to inquire about becoming a consultant," she said.

"I'm on the other line. Can I call you later? Please give me your phone number," I lied to her.

I wrote her number and we hung up. I had no idea what a *consultant* was! Right away I called Tema, my mentor. She would be able to explain what a consultant was. I told her about the recent call from Pam. "Brilliant!" Tema exclaimed, as she was pondering my spontaneous and witty response. "Why say no before knowing whether or not I was in front of a new opportunity?" I explained to her.

Tema described the Mary Kay modality, where representatives called consultants sold for the brand through private parties. If I was interested in pursuing that kind of business model it would entail a more sophisticated organization, with commissions, different levels among the vendors, coaching and motivation. She offered her help to assemble the package and guide me during the execution.

If I Could be Several Marianas!

I could not have been more grateful. How many opportunities there were! Every day I had more ideas, and more marketing opportunities. And so, in the following months, we developed a project that engaged more than fifty consultants selling throughout the country.

To handle all this, I dedicated a room next to the entrance in our house where I established my first permanent store. Here people could come and buy my products after having met us in some of the many places where we popped up with our nomad store. The room was small and cute. I displayed a few collections arranging them by colors or specific themes. White opal jewelry paired with a shawl in turquoise tones, complemented by a white briefcase created the marine set. The last touch was giant shells t from Uruguay to evoke the ocean feel.

The evening set consisted of gold *bijoux, a light*, black scarf with metallic golden threads, a very chic evening bag embellished with gold buttons, and an antique elegant watch to finish the set. It was definitely a sight to behold. I placed scented candles next to each set to entice customers with all their senses

Later that year, Eli built a warehouse in the basement of our house to store merchandise, and slowly, as money permitted, he continued the project building on the other end of the basement, a beautiful and bigger store. We worked non-stop, and the need for extra help was soon here. As soon as we started to look into hiring, Alice showed up in our lives.

Alice, my Guardian Angel

Alice was a small woman who worked helping me with all the tasks of the store with incredible speed. Her children were in the Philippines with her husband and, according to the current immigration program, it would take five to six years to bring her family to Canada. I never heard her complaining, I never saw her upset. Once we got to know her better, we suggested she live with us to help her save on rent and food.

She accepted gratefully. Every day, Alice would get up very early, prepare coffee for the two of us, and start working. She always found something to do. After a year of living with us and working hard carrying boxes, pricing stock, selling and cleaning the silver jewelry, she opened her heart to me and shared her story, "Mariana, my children are the most important people in my life. I am here for them, to offer them a better future. I had a nice life in the Philippines, I was a school principal for many years where I earned the respect of colleagues, students and parents. I had a hefty salary. My husband is the police chief of our town. We could have stayed there, but we aspire to more promising opportunities for our children."

At that time, she also revealed that the main reason she went to bed early was because every morning she woke up at four to do homework on Skype with her little ones and read them stories before bed. I was in shock. The sacrifices Alice made for her children were immeasurable. I have never met a devoted mother like her. Alice's attitude was phenomenal, always positive and thankful for the opportunities presented to her. Her desire to excel knew no limits.

She never looked for my sympathy or felt self-pity so I wasn't sure why she decided to share all this at this particular time. Later I understood that she needed to find encouragement to make her big announcement; a month later she would go to the Philippines to visit her family.

Her plan wasn't going for twenty days as was determined by law; she was going for three months. "If you can't wait for me or if you want to terminate my contract, I would understand," she said seriously. Then she continued, "Sorry Mariana, there is nothing

Say YES, Ask questions later

to discuss, those are my priorities. I am sorry for disappointing you. I will never forget your generosity and I really care for you although my family comes first."

I was frozen. How would I survive three months without Alice? She was my right hand and, as I liked to say, she was my left foot too.

I remained silent, in stupor. After a few seconds I was able to see the bigger picture. How could I be so selfish thinking about myself and my needs? Her children needed her much more than me! I had to be grateful for all this wonderful woman did for me and my business. She gave me 200% and worked as if the business was her own. I raised my head and said confidently, "You are right Alice, you and your family deserve it. I applaud you for the decision. I will be waiting for you at your return. I'm very thrilled for you. Go and enjoy your family."

She looked at me relieved and grateful. She ran to me and hugged me while she jumped like a little girl, shouting, "Thank you, thank you, thank you!"

That night I told Eli how much I admired Alice for her clarity and determination. She knew her priorities. She was a pure and honest woman, the epitome of motherhood. I felt asleep thinking how grateful I was to have her in my life as an example to follow and learn from.

Be Different

The business was moving from strong to stronger. Sales were increasing, and we began to import containers of handbags. The garage was transformed into the new warehouse, the same as the room that had been the first "store." The basement was completely rebuilt into a fabulous department store.

As clients came down the stairs, it was funny to see their jaw drop while screaming, "*Oh, my gosh!* This is a hidden paradise of handbags. Amazing!"

It was a time of endless hours of work, much effort and much learning. I begged Eli to quit taxi driving and help me with the business. Wisely he answered, "My salary pays the bills. If two years in a row you can generate your salary and mine, I'll quit without hesitation."

I asked, "And why two years?"

"Because the first year could be a coincidence," he answered. "The second one means you have something bigger on your hands, a real business."

He was cautious, calculated and poised. He didn't allow me to wrap him up in my inordinate passion. His thoughts were sensible, giving me peace of mind. We became a perfect team. He managed the finances of the house, while I, full of ideas, made the business grow and contributed more and more income for him to invest and administer.

By the end of the second year, numbers far exceeded expectations.

Say YES, Ask questions later

Eli sold his taxi and started working at the company.

For the year end we decided to have a private party at our house. The main theme of the party would be Turkey, since we had traveled to Istanbul and brought home a spectacular selection of handmade pewter jewelry. It was a good opportunity to thank our customers for the support they had offered and to present the new collection. We hired a belly dancer and Eli cooked traditional Turkish food. We invited many people without knowing what to expect. According to some experienced business owners, usually only ten percent of the invitees could be expected to attend. The event was planned as an *open house.* We would be open from ten in the morning until six o'clock in the evening and people would come and go during those hours.

Thankfully Alice was back and helped Eli and me get all ready for the party. After a week of arduous work, the store looked divine. We printed more than a thousand pamphlets that Flor and Rebecca distributed around the neighborhood. At ten on the dot the first group of ladies arrived. Some came for the first time and were speechless. They ate, they drank, they bought, they chatted, and nobody wanted to leave. Clients continued to arrive throughout the day and once there, they were so in "awe" that we heard them calling their friends inviting them to join the experience.

Everyone indulged themselves with the delights Eli had prepared. The Turkish jewelry was an outstanding success. The dancer was engaging, having the crowd dancing with her. The food Eli prepared wasn't enough. The number of customers that showed up exceeded our expectations by far. Without hesitation, while the party was at its height, Eli started cooking in front of the surprised guests. That by itself was quite a scene!

Women went up and down the stairs from the store into the kitchen, and, while eating something, they shared among themselves the treasures found in their last expedition into the store. Enticed by the discovery of others, they would return downstairs to explore for more discoveries.

It was seven in the evening when the last client departed.

As we looked at each other, Alice, Eli and I, we were exhausted and ecstatic at the same time. "Incredible!" said Alice. "More than a hundred people came through the door."

We could not believe what had happened. We made more than one hundred and twenty transactions. Eli enjoyed counting and tidying up the bills while Alice and I commented on the popular items sold and some funny anecdotes happened with customers during the day. It was a unique experience and absolutely unforgettable.

Say YES, Ask questions later

The next day we continued receiving phone calls from new and old customers inquiring if the following Sunday we would be open again. After hearing the incredible stories from their friends, they wanted to experience this themselves. Even if we wanted to do it again, we couldn't. We were extremely tired and at the verge of exhaustion. We needed time to recover so we invited them to join us the next year. After that, our themed parties were one hallmark of the company.

Each year the theme was inspired by the most recently visited country, from where we would bring a selection of products and many stories to share. Eli learned the cuisine of the country, shared recipes and delighted our customers. Without knowing, we had created a remarkable experience that people would remember for many years ahead. There was nothing like it in Edmonton or anywhere else nearby.

CHAPTER 8

More Growth

"I'm going to order two hundred purses of this style that are selling like hot cakes," I stated matter-of-factly.

"Why so many? Why don't you sell what you have?" asked Eli.

"Because the ones I have are for winter. I need spring colors, new things."

"Do what you want." He sounded disappointed.

"Why are you upset?" I inquired

"Because you have a lot of stock and you keep adding more and more merchandise." I sensed that was not the real problem. Eli was not enjoying having so many people going in and out of the house. I loved it. As a matter of fact, I felt I had a piece of Uruguay in Edmonton.

Later in the day I asked him for help. "Will you help me load the car?"

I heard a deep, long sigh, then Eli said, "I can't deal with this anymore." He sounded serious. "It's time to get more help."

Sharon came into our lives.

Sharon was lively and cheerful. She came from Manila, where she worked in the fashion and television industry. With Sharon's arrival, we felt relieved. We worked in two teams: Alice with me and Sharon with Eli. Eli drove Sharon to the sites where our pop-up store was scheduled. He loaded and unloaded the van and he was in charge of handling the money. Eli didn't know or care about the products and neither did he have the patience to serve customers. On the other hand, Sharon was similar to me. She loved to sell and engage with the customers. Every day she was becoming better at her craft. She knew every detail of the infinite purses we carried. She knew the compartments, the strap's length, and every hidden zipper. Observing customers preferences, she learned what to offer to each one with precision.

I was pleased to team up with Alice. Selling was definitely not her thing; although she loved to do everything I didn't like. She was well organized, full of energy and loved handling money.

Sharon soon moved to live with us. She originally came to Canada as a caregiver to support her son with special needs. The salary Sharon earned in the Philippines was not enough to offer the best therapies for him.

"Once again," I thought, "when it comes to rescuing their family, *nothing* is impossible for these lioness women."

With time, Eli and I were transformed into a kind of adoptive parents for Sharon.

In Philipino culture, the elder person is always the authority, and Sharon respected Alice for it, but it also worked out beautifully for work. Sharon and Alice were opposites: Alice was serious, Sharon was playful, Alice neat and organized, Sharon creative and messy. We grew into a team that worked harmoniously. Alice organized, Eli administered, Sharon executed, and I created.

While everyone was happy with their tasks, tensions decreased, and the business continued to grow by leaps and bounds. Absorbed by growth, difficulties and achievements, the first five years of the company were gone in no time.

Purses in my Kitchen. NO!

Eli opened the kitchen cabinet to take out a pot. "Whose purse is this? What is a purse doing with my pots?"

"It's mine, I hid it because a customer came, and I didn't want it to look messy," I said, dismissing the matter.

"I cannot take it anymore! There are purses everywhere! We don't have a house anymore! Soon I will not have a place to sleep because you will also use our bed. Is it not enough with the garage, the basement and the entrance room? What is the limit? Not in my kitchen! Purses in my kitchen? No!" He repeated, as if trying to convince himself, "It's time to move the business out of the house. This is no longer an option. I want my house back!"

Say YES, Ask questions later

I understood that the time had come to move despite not wanting to. I was comfortable in the house, allowing me to stay close to Flor. Eli was not kidding, however. The next week he went looking for a place. The list of requirements was strict and extended. It had to be close to home, large enough to accommodate all our inventory, easily accessible and with enough parking for our customers.

After months of searching, Eli finally found what we needed. It was more than we wanted to invest, but, as my dad always said, "It is always necessary to owe in order to keep growing." So, with great enthusiasm we threw ourselves into the deep end of the pool.

We painted, moved furniture, bought exhibitors, and finally organized the space to have a large warehouse and a small showroom in case some customers wanted to come by. It was never our intention to open a retail store to the public, since I didn't want to be tied to a set schedule.

The Giant Purse

"Eli, I have a great idea."

He looked at me with a face that said, "Now what?"

"Do you realize that our place is the only one in the complex that has double height? What do you think if we put a luminous sign in the shape of a giant purse, a violet giant purse same as our trademark snakeskin handbags? Imagine it illuminated! Everyone will see it!"

"Good idea, but... that must be very expensive! Can we do something simpler, something temporary so we do not incur more expenses??"

I wasn't ready to take a "no" for an answer, so I proceeded. "We need to attract new customers. Over time, sales will pay for the sign and more!"

"Find out the price and we'll see," said Eli thinking I would forget about this crazy idea.

The next week I had three estimates. I was fascinated with the idea. I could see the purse illuminated in an intense violet. Everyone would talk about our sign. We presented the giant purse project to the condominium administration. They told us they thought there would be no problem and that they would respond to us in the coming weeks.

A few weeks later I asked Eli, "Have you talked to the president of the Condo board? What are we going to do about our sign?"

"Our messages are not being answered. I've already sent him emails, letters, and nothing!" Eli said indignantly. In the meantime, the giant sign was ready, but without permission we didn't want to have it installed. It ended up sitting in our back room.

Six months later, a big shipment of purses was about to arrive, and we needed the space the giant purse was taking.

Say YES, Ask questions later

"What to do?" I asked Eli, "I don't know where to put those boxes!"

"We have given them enough time to respond," said Eli. "Today I'm going to call the company to install it."

On Monday morning they installed the sign. It was spectacular! The intense violet color stood out against the yellowish and insipid façade of the condominium. All of our neighbors came to see it and to praise us for the initiative. "What a great idea! So original! It's going to attract a lot of people to our strip mall," they said.

When we opened the store on Tuesday, we found a letter under the door from the administrator of the condominium. The same person who failed to respond to any of our hundreds of letters, emails and phone messages for the last six months. Suddenly, the day after the sign was installed, they had taken the time to write and personally bring the letter. The letter expressed their indignation at seeing the sign installed without having received authorization from the president nor waiting for the response of the administration. That letter didn't clarify the reason why they had not answered anything in six months— six months of absolute silence!

They instructed us to immediately remove the sign and forbade us to put it back up.

"How unfortunate! I'm not going to take anything out! Eli, it seems to me that we have to go talk to the president."

"Calm down my love, you cannot go talk to anyone. The only thing missing is smoke coming out of your ears. We cannot fight. They are our neighbors." As always Eli was the only one capable of convincing me to see reason

The next day, when I was calmer, Eli and I went to talk to the president. His secretary was sitting in the reception area. After she announced us to her boss, instead of letting us in, the man came out to greet us. In a dismissive tone he said, "I can see you don't understand English well. Didn't I tell you to wait for our decision? The bylaws clearly say that the exterior walls of your bay are owned by the condominium, but you still installed your sign." Mocking our immigrant status, he added, "In case you cannot read English either, I can explain what that means." And almost shouting, he ordered, "That sign has to get out of there! It is on property that is not yours. Do you understand now?"

The tall-rude-man had managed to get Eli extremely angry. Eli wanted to hit him.

"Calm down, Eliko. It is not worth getting into trouble for such an ignorant person! Justice always comes...even for immigrants who don't understand English well," I begged.

Say YES, Ask questions later

That night I called Tema. She suggested we contact a television program dedicated to intervening in conflicts between neighbors, and our story would surely interest them. "If you agree, I will write a press release and send it to all the media. The public in Edmonton likes to express their opinions. Maybe it will help to convince the owner that the sign would contribute to highlighting this strip mall, which is totally lost within the urban landscape," she remarked.

The next morning, we were on the centre page of the *Edmonton Sun,* a major local newspaper. The members of the condo association's board were outraged. They sent us emails threatening to take us to trial for defamation. All of Edmonton now knew about our famous sign. People came to the store to offer their solidarity and a signature in support. We became famous for the 'giant purse'.

What people didn't know was that for countless nights we didn't sleep while we worked with expensive lawyers to help us understand the condominium bylaws. I felt discouraged and I wanted to get out of the location. I didn't know how to deal with such arrogant people. What deeply anguished me was finding myself at a disadvantage because my English was not fluent enough to understand the legal vocabulary used in this matter.

Eli was outraged by the way we were treated, and the injustice we were enduring. This motivated him to take his time to do some investigating. Soon he learned the administrator was family related to the president, so a conflict of interest was present. There were also many financial irregularities, and little by little Eli talked to the neighbors, shared the information he had obtained and learned that people didn't attend meetings because this man was detested by the majority of them. Nobody wanted to see him or argue with him.

Eli organized a general assembly. Nine people showed up, plus Eli.

The meeting began, and the president asked, "Any new business?"

"Yes, I want to vote for the president's resignation," said Eli, seriously.

Everyone looked at him in amazement.

"And how do you plan to do that?" the president answered angrily

Eli drew seventeen proxies from neighbors who had authorized him to vote on their behalf. The president paled. The tension was unbearable. Eli continued calm and firm, "Nobody wants a president who compromises members of the board by making them sign blank cheques even though they don't know what the cheques are for. Nor do they want a president who is so dishonest that he hires relatives with ridiculous, exaggerated salaries, one who mistreats women and immigrants."

The president stood up and angrily replied, "This is outrageous. I volunteered for years for the

Say YES, Ask questions later

condominium when nobody wanted to take charge, and this is what I have to hear from this ...?"

Eli interrupted him, "From this immigrant?" He proceeded: "At this moment I would like to present a motion to remove the president from his position. Secretary, do you take note? We are eighteen in favor of the resignation of the president." He handed the powers of attorney documents to the secretary. "Anyone else in favor?" Four more hands shot up, and Eli continued, "Against?" Five hands were raised, including that of the president. Eli interrupted, "If I am well informed, the president cannot vote since he didn't pay the last three months of common expenses. Is that correct, Secretary?" She nodded fearfully, and Eli continued, "I am afraid this is also part of the bylaws, and this time we are going to do things legally. As you can see, I understand some English."

"Twenty-two in favor, four against," the secretary summed up. "According to the co-ownership regulations, the president is removed from his position."

Eli stood up and said, "I raise the motion to vote for a new board and a new president. Does anyone object?" The room was silent.

Alice and her Family

That morning Alice came into the store squeaking and jumping, even more cheerful than usual. "The papers came! My family can finally come to Canada! The suffering is over!"

"This has to be celebrated. When will they come? Are you going to fly back home to help them pack up?"

Alice could hardly speak as she was extremely emotional. Her plan was to travel in mid-April for a month to close up the house and return with them. "I need you to help me rent a place by the time they arrive," she begged.

"No, Alice. Rent? No! You have to buy."

She replied, "You think so? I don't dare. It is too much responsibility. I am afraid."

"Come on, Alice, what are you afraid of? We will support you. If you don't qualify for a mortgage, we'll co-sign as your guarantors."

"No, no. I don't like that. You already have given me too much and I am almost sure they won't approve me for a mortgage."

"How do you know, if you have never asked for it? Don't look at the final price of the property. Look at the monthly payment. You will not believe it, but the monthly payment is often cheaper than paying rent. Let me call Yanina to start looking for something to see this weekend. And I will call the bank, to see what documents they need."

"But I need to talk to my husband, see what he thinks."

Say YES, Ask questions later

Her husband thought it was an excellent idea. He knew we would offer them the best advice to move forward. So that weekend we went to see houses. On Monday, Alice presented the papers at the bank. They rejected her credit application. "And now what?"

"Now we try another bank. That's how it works, Alice. Remember, the rule is to never give up."

By Friday she already had a mortgage pre-approved and had an offer on a house. The offer didn't work out, so we continued looking for properties in the following weeks.

Finally, she found the perfect property, in the location she wanted, and at an excellent price.

"Alice, do you need an advance for your legal expenses?"

"No thanks. I have everything calculated. I saved enough for the down payment and the lawyer's fees."

"What about air tickets for everyone and the immigration fees?"

"Everything is under control," Alice answered proudly.

I had known this woman for five years and I had never seen her spend anything superfluously, not even for a coffee or a ticket to the movies. Nothing! She wore clothes given to her by her sister-in-law, or me. Every penny she earned she kept and administered meticulously. Now that the moment had finally arrived, she had everything under control! This was Alice; everything in perfect order, neat and calculated.

My spontaneity made her nervous the same as her rigidity scared me, but with time, we learned to appreciate the value in our differences. Alice started slowly buying things for the house. Every time there was a sale, there she was. Everything she bought she kept in a corner in the store. When it was time to travel, she had some sheets, pillows and a double inflatable mattress, plus some little things for the kitchen.

We took possession of Alice's house while she went to pick up her family. One afternoon, while walking through the empty house, I thought of this wise woman so deliciously simple and disciplined. I remembered a time when Alice asked me if I would get angry if she didn't return to Canada after one of her visits to the Philippines. "How could I get angry?" I remember replying to her, "Of course I would understand! Actually, I was really struggling to understand how you endured being so far away from your children for so long." She, with tears in her eyes, explained to me, "My sacrifice is worth it for my loved-ones to have the opportunities that I didn't." We cried together with our hearts clenched in pain and emotion.

Mother's Day was approaching, and I planned to organize an event in the store. "Why not honour Alice?" That night I wrote a heart-to-heart letter to our loyal clientele, asking for help. I shared the story of this wonderful woman who became a soul-sister and who taught me by her example what true motherhood was. I shared how I watched her sacrifice not for a day or two, but for five consecutive years without highs or lows, without confusion or temptation, with a behavior almost impossible to reproduce. I shared how she proudly managed to save penny over penny to buy her own house and bring all the members of her family to Canada without asking for help. The only thing she had not saved enough for was furniture. I appealed to the solidarity of the women, whom Alice had served with her best smile throughout, to help me furnish her house.

The next morning, I received a torrent of calls and messages answering my letter. People thanked me for sharing the story and allowing them to be part of it. For two days we received items non-stop for Alice and her family's new home. Once we finished our workdays, we went out with Sharon and her brother until midnight to pick donations around the city. We loaded chairs, desks, computers. It was incredible to witness what was happening! People wanted to help, and I was grateful and excited!

I spent two days in the house arranging everything. Clients and friends showed up. Some provided personal care products such as shampoo, soap, creams and more. Others donated games for Alice's young son, and new appliances came in boxes. There were sheets, towels, crockery, more furniture, a TV, and a computer. One client provided new mattresses for each member of the family after the company where she worked learned about Alice's story. Another client donated a supermarket gift certificate enough to fill the refrigerator and pantry. At ten o'clock in the evening of the second day, the house was equipped. I sat down and looked around, when I realized that it looked like a magazine house: paintings, lamps, flowers, all coordinated with an exquisite taste. I was exhausted, but my heart was full of happiness and gratitude.

The next day I left on a trip overseas with my daughter. Sharon was in charge of buying dinner and waiting for Alice and her family in the house, taking pictures, and documenting everything.

According to Sharon, when they entered their new home, they couldn't believe it. They opened the cabinets, and they ran from room to room shouting out what they were discovering. The only thing that was missing was their clothes and their toothbrushes; there was toothpaste too! Alice looked in shock and said, "I'm going to kill Mariana! I'm sure she spent a fortune and I'll have to work overtime to pay her."

When Sharon told her what had really happened, Alice couldn't stop crying and thanking everyone.

Growing Pains

We needed more staff as customers were coming to the store more often than we predicted. We also understood the need to establish regular business

Say YES, Ask questions later

hours. The demand for our products increased. Every day we were invited to new places! Sometimes we needed to say no, which as you might know by now, was against all my beliefs. To fulfill our customers' demand, we decided to put together a third team.

We sponsored Gerardo, who arrived from Mexico with his wife and three children. We sponsored Kika, a vivacious young woman with her beautiful daughter Emilia. Still wasn't enough! Later we had hired Canadians and also had the opportunity to sponsor people from Israel, Croatia, Spain, Uruguay. I believed in immigrants. They were hungry and ambitious, and brought with them valuable skills. I was giving them the opportunity that was so hard for me to get at the beginning, when no one knows who you are and what you can offer. It truly felt like the United Nations which gave the business a special sense of community and diversity, embracing accents and life stories. Marlene was a client who used to come every weekend religiously and sometimes, if she couldn't resist, in the middle of the week. She would come to the counter and ask me gently, "Mariana, could you scarf me up?". During her visits she never missed the opportunity to help a client or share a story about the endless compliments she would receive when wearing our pieces.

On one of her visits, I asked her jokingly, "Why don't you work with us? I can see you really enjoy being around."

"I would love to," she replied. "Can I start today?"

"Of course! You are hired."

We laughed out loud, "Let's talk about money!"

"I'm not interested, " she replied, seriously I want to work here because I love the vibe of the place. I have my nine to five job Monday to Friday. This is just for fun."

And that's how Marlene joined the family for the next three years. We called her Nana, because she became the grandmother we all needed, filling the role wonderfully.

Now we had a storefront, wholesale clients, private events in our premises during the evenings, and three teams out in different locations every day. It was a big and complicated operation with logistics nobody but Eli, Alice and I understood. I no longer had the time to venture out to sell or to sew my beautiful scarves. I needed to learn how to outsource from India, Europe, South America or China.

My days went fast ordering new products, organizing work schedules, finding enough events/venues to keep all the teams busy, making sure each had what they needed. At night, when everybody was sleeping, I ran the marketing for the business while learning new strategies to stay on top. I recognized the need of an online store to serve customers located in the remote areas of the province.

There were days I wouldn't see Flor or Eli. Business was booming, and I didn't want to lose momentum. I was passionate about watching women having fun and playing like little girls. I loved everything I was doing, and I was doing very well.

The Real-Life Skills University

The work team had grown, and we were already fourteen members, including Eli and me. I admit that I was not an easy boss. I was tough and demanding while fair and generous at the same time. It was hard for me to understand the motivations of some of the workers, a concern that I didn't know how to resolve. I had no experience managing others. I thought everybody had the same work ethics, and common sense. Experience was proving me wrong and I needed some help. I phoned Tema. "I needed your opinion", so we agreed to meet for lunch the next day. "How can it be that with fourteen people I have so many problems? What do others do with hundreds of employees? The problem must be me," I told Tema as we ate.

"I don't think so. I would say that it is a common issue entrepreneurs face. Every time I interview CEO's or business owners, they tell me their biggest challenge is the staff. You should listen to a *podcast* of ..."

"A what?" I interrupted sharply. "What is that?"

"A *podcast* is an online recording. Like a radio show, but you can listen to it at any time."

"And how is it done? Can you explain to me, please?"

"You download an application called…" Tema continued to give me the instructions. That's how our conversations always played out. I took notes, later when I got home, researched and integrated it into the business. I loved it. Tema was a walking digital marketing encyclopedia.

"Returning to the matter of employees," Tema knew how to keep me on topic when I got distracted, which was very often. "Is there an entrepreneur in our city you admire when it comes to managing staff?"

"The owner of the Italian Center. Teresa is her name, isn't it?" I asked doubtfully.

"Yes, Teresa Spinelli. She is growing a lot lately. She owns two supermarkets and is opening another one soon. I heard she will have more than five hundred employees with their expansion. Why don't we call her to ask her opinion?"

"I don't know her. Do you know her? Also, I imagine she is a very busy person."

"You never know. She likes to support other women entrepreneurs. What can we lose by calling her? The worst she can say is no."

Tema was right. There was nothing to lose. I didn't know Teresa personally, but I attended a conference where she was the keynote speaker she had seemed

Say YES, Ask questions later

like a very generous and intelligent woman. Tema had her personal phone number and she dialled on the spot. I heard Tema saying, "Thank you Teresa, tomorrow at ten, at the downtown location. Yes, I am coming with Mariana. See you tomorrow." We had a date with Teresa Spinelli. I was over the moon! Then Tema said, "Do you know what is the funniest? If you hadn't named her, I would not have thought of her. She's a very special lady. I should interview her for my next podcast on customer service!"

"Tomorrow I will pick you up," I announced to Tema. I won't be able to sleep tonight. It's like having an interview with the Beatles! And you got it in five minutes! When I grow up, I want to be like you and Teresa Spinelli." We laughed. Tema knew how to push me forward. We were for sure a great team.

The meeting with Teresa was incredible. I felt as if I had known her for many years. Anyone could tell she was Italian by watching her for a few minutes. She spoke loud and fast, waving her hands constantly. As usual, food was part of the equation. As soon as she joined us, she ordered paninis and coffee for us. Her eyes were deep and attentive, but what attracted me most about this woman was her overflowing generosity and sense of practicality. She was focused, with a clear goal, and nothing would stop her; she wanted to positively impact as many lives as possible promoting change and growth. She wanted to see the life of her staff's families advance and improve. She was open to share her experience, her knowledge and wisdom. She always made time to support another community project that was presented to her. I understood that her secret was not taking things personally. In her own words, "I can only be responsible for what I do. I know I deliver from my heart. What each one does with what I give is up to them to decide. We rarely know what others are immersed in at the time of receiving. Only where they are will define if they will receive happily or bitterly. There was a lot of wisdom in her words. Throughout the following year I learned more about her entrepreneurial journey. After the sudden passing of her brother and dad, she was faced with the challenge of taking charge of a family business that was bigger than she could have imagined. Employees who had worked with her father for more than thirty years wondered how this young lady would run the business. Her performance exceeded their expectations. Not only did she continue her father's business with responsibility, she took it to a whole new level. Soon she became one of the top hundred most successful women entrepreneurs in the province and was indicted in the Hall of Fame of Edmonton! The tough lessons made her grow stronger and gain the respect of her staff and the whole community. Caring, compassion, and straight-forward personality are few of the many skills which made her become loved by so many! Teresa always gives from her heart.

Teresa is a role model to me. As time went by, we got to know each other on a personal level, giving me the opportunity to get her wise perspective on everyday life topics. I believe this woman is a gift to society. Her business is what I call a University of real-life skills enhancing the lives of her staff and the communities they are serving.

The Academic World

I went with Tema to the Faculty Club at the University of Alberta. In one corner sat a woman who caught my attention. She wore crimson red catlike glasses, matching red lipstick and a colorful necklace with giant colored balls that stood out above her parrot green top. "Who is she?" I asked Tema.

"Sandra. You're going to love her. She is the Director of the Edmonton Public School Foundation." We approached the corner and Tema addressed her, "Hello, Sandra, long time no see! Allow me to introduce Mariana, the owner of Princess Florence. This is a business that you must get to know. I am sure you will love it. You will find accessories from all over the world."

Immediately Sandra got up and asked me amicably, "Where is the store? How come I don't know it?"

"It's relatively new. We are mobile," I said.

"Where is that accent so...?"

I noticed that she was looking for the right word.

But spontaneous and fresh as she is, she threw out an honest, "So...sexy!" And she imitated me with a deep and sensual voice while adding, "If you don't do well with your accessories, you can always have a *sex line*. You would be excellent!"

Tema laughed, agreed, then they laughed together and changed the topic.

"What an occurrence!" I thought. "How easygoing! She just met me and told me that!" It was not usual. This woman had a special charisma that hypnotized. She spoke very quickly and every word that came out of her mouth was intelligent and shrewd. I interrupted and exaggerated my sexy and husky voice, I said very seriously, "I would love to collaborate with the Foundation. Could we do something together? Maybe something like *sexy calls for kids*? We would have a lot of press!" I added ironically.

Sandra and Tema could not stop laughing at my joke. She immediately gave me her card and told me to call her on Monday at nine. I called her on Monday. We laughed for a while and then I put forward my idea. She would invite the teachers to the store, and I would treat them with Turkish food that Eli would prepare. Out of the total sales for the day, I would give her a percentage for the Foundation.

She asked me, "What do you need from me?"

"Nothing; simply invite people."

We selected a date near Christmas.

The party was an absolute success. Her wit and humor attracted her colleagues like honey to a bee.

Her main focus in life has been to make sure every kid could access education. She created the foundation in order to supply nutritious breakfast to kids in the inner city. She wholeheartedly believed, the most powerful tool we can offer a child is Education. I have never met someone who has devoted her life for a cause the way Sandra has. She would speak her mind regardless of the criticism or judgment of others. She was always clear, focused and moving forward. Every fundraising event in support of the foundation I attended in the coming years, was a piece of art! One funnier and more creative than the one before. Kid's art was featured in ways I have never seen again since, and her public recognition of each and every one of the supporters disregarding the size of the check donated was heartwarming.

"Try not to exhaust yourself, it is better to keep moving forward slowly and steady and never stop giving," she would say, and "*Kiss and release, and never give up.*"

Fame and Ego

Today, as I look back, I realize that during the chaos of work, I lost my center of balance. The business had transformed into a life of its own and didn't have any limits. I was neglecting my body and my soul, again. More importantly, I was neglecting my family. They were screaming for my attention, but I was deaf. I was blinded by success and fame. I was trapped in a whirlpool that absorbed me, made me addicted to the same adrenaline, which was preventing me from resting most of my nights. I was a bundle of nerves, exaltation and full of my own ego.

I had been here before. Back in Uruguay while running my real estate company I had worn myself out, and although I told myself I had learned my lesson, clearly this was not the case. I was doing exactly the same!

Human behavior is like a river. It tends to flow back to the old known bed. Opening a new path takes years of wind and rain eroding the rock on a daily basis. I realized it was time to make consistent efforts to regain balance in my life to leave the old and toxic path forever.

CHAPTER 9

The Surgery

"Ma, my ankles hurt a lot," Flor told me that morning.

I called her at noon. "I arranged an appointment with the doctor for today at five. Can you make it?"

"Yes. I will be back from school, so we can go." We arrived at Dr. Jablonski's office. It always smelled good. We were invited to go straight in. He knocked at the door a few minutes later.

"Hello! What a pleasure to see you! How are you? So long! How big you are, Flor! How tall! What brings you here? How can I help?"

"I have been sore for a while but recently my knees have begun to hurt as well." He examined her in detail.

"I do not see anything to worry about. They are growing pains, but for greater safety I would like you to see a sports doctor. If I remember correctly, you dance ballet and sometimes some movements can cause pain."

We visited a sports doctor, then a physiotherapist and later a pain therapist. Nobody was able to find the cause of the afflictions which were growing in Flor's body. She felt increasingly frustrated and her discontent was becoming more and more evident.

One day, after a very stressful visit to a doctor who suggested doing all kinds of invasive treatments to intervene with her knee, we decided to go back to Dr. Jablonski. We told him that we still had not found a solution to the problem and that we wanted to see a rheumatologist.

"A rheumatologist? Why?"

"Because in Uruguay, when your body hurts, you go to a rheumatologist," I said a little impatiently.

He arranged for an appointment with a rheumatologist. Unfortunately, we had to wait three months. On the designated date, we entered Children's Hospital and went straight to Dr. Leblanc's office. Her nurse performed a number of physical tests: bending Flor's body to the front, to the side and then back. She left the room without commenting on her findings. Flor and I looked at each other. The door opened, and a middle-aged woman came into the room. She was wearing a very white tunic and carried a stethoscope with children's drawings. Smiling, she introduced herself and kindly asked Flor to stand and walk normally towards the back of the room. She watched her from behind, told her to come back, and watched her walk head on.

"My dear, you are crooked!" she exclaimed. "Surely it's scoliosis. Has anyone ever told you?"

Flor explained some other symptoms of her suffering. The doctor listened attentively and determined, "Let's start right now. We'll take some Xrays and we'll do some special studies. I would like to rule out some possibilities."

After an entire day waiting and wandering around, we returned to Dr. Leblanc's office. She came in with a folder full of papers. While she silently read the results of the analyses, I felt tired but relieved. I will not deny that I was afraid of what the results might show, but finally someone had ventured to find the root of the problem.

Flor was restless. It had been a long day. Finally, the doctor raised her head and spoke, "The good news is that we could discard a lot of things that worried me. As I thought, it's scoliosis. The curve is an S and is 23 degrees. There is also some rotation at the top. When the spine is bent, the body compensates and that is why the knees and ankles begin to hurt. Hip pains are also part of the same. I'm going to refer you to a surgeon."

My blood ran cold. "And a corset?" I interrupted.

"That is used before girls have their first period, to prevent the curve from continuing to increase. As Flor has already passed that stage, the corset is not an option for her. Dr. Moreau is the head of surgery for the scoliosis team. He will determine if surgical intervention is necessary. You will be in very good hands." And looking at my daughter, she added, "Flor, you have behaved like a champion. Any questions?"

Flor shook her head. Fear flooded her eyes. I hugged her and squeezed her hard against me.

"You must be very tired," the doctor continued, handing me her card. She added, "I imagine that tomorrow you will have new questions. On the card you will find my private phone number and my email. Do not hesitate to contact me. And you too, Flor, if you need to talk, call me." While she was accompanying us to the door, she gave Flor a little book and pointed out, "Here is some basic information. But on the internet, you will find much more. There are some scoliosis forums that I recommend. There you will meet girls of your age from all over the world who are going through the same thing. You are not alone! And on top of that and, most important, you have your mom!"

I got emotional. The woman's words radiated a humanity that I did not remember having felt in many years. I missed Uruguay. We left holding hands. "What do you think?" I asked my daughter.

"Well, at least we know what I have."

"Are you afraid?"

"A little, but I don't want to live with pain."

I knew what she was talking about. I lived my whole life with pain, and it was not good. I wanted to cry. I was afraid, but I had to be strong for Flor. She needed me more than ever. I looked at my phone. Eli had called me five times.

An Angel Came into our Lives

Sarah was the nurse. Her voice was sweet and serene. She was blonde, blue-eyed with delicate features and a broad smile.

Dr. Moreau was tall, with little hair, hard features, and wore a light blue tunic. It had been six months since the last consultation with the rheumatologist. The curve had increased to 35 degrees. The pain intensified, and depression was taking over Flor. I was desperate. Without many words, Moreau checked her. He sat down, wrote something on his computer and specified, without looking at us, addressing Flor, "First you have to lose weight and strengthen your abdominal muscles. We will see in the next three months if the curve continues to move forward." Then he ordered Sarah to coordinate the appointment and book a new X-ray. He stood up and added, "Any questions?"

We had thousands of questions, but his coldness took us by surprise. Flor reacted, "Does this cure itself?"

Without any expression on his face, he said, "There are exercises that help prevent the curve from advancing. The surgery corrects the curvature in a definitive way. In general, if the curve doesn't exceed 50 degrees, I prefer not to operate."

"And the pains? What do I do?"

"Physiotherapy and as many abdominals as you can. I'm not a friend of medication. Sarah will better explain it to you. Anything else?"

"No, thanks," I mumbled, stunned. I felt that the doctor was speaking to us as if he wanted us to leave.

He shook hands with us. When he reached the door, he turned and said with a half-smile, "Next time I want you to look thin like a gazelle," and left with Sarah for a moment.

Flor was angry and offended. "Ma, did we wait so many months for this? And what do I do with the pain? He doesn't understand me! All he has to say to me is to lose weight? Couldn't he have been a little more understanding and kind?"

Sarah entered. She saw the tears in Flor's eyes. She came over and put her arms around her. Almost whispering, she gently said, "Dr. Moreau is the best surgeon in scoliosis in the province of Alberta. Can you keep a secret?"

Flor nodded.

"I know he is not sympathetic, but he has golden hands. Trust me. The wait is worth it. An operation is something very serious, with many risks. He prefers to avoid surgeries as much as possible. I will not let you suffer. Will you trust me? I'll give you some ideas for your pain and I'll give you my cell phone number, so you can call or text me anytime you have a question."

Flor smiled. Sarah gave her what she had come for.

Say YES, Ask questions later

Hard News

We arrived at the hospital to monitor the condition of her spine. Physiotherapy had not helped at all. The pains continued and my daughter's mood deteriorated day by day. We went to the x-ray room. Susana, a Latin customer from the store, assisted Flor with extra patience and affection. She could not tell us the results, but I understood by the look on her face that something was not right. We went up the elevator. We entered a waiting room full of children and teenagers. We waited impatiently until Sarah's smile showed through the huge glass that separated the office. We were invited in. She knew how to treat Flor. As we walked to the office she asked if she was still doing ballet and told her that she herself had been a dancer for many years. Sarah's softness contrasted with the severity of the surgeon's face.

The doctor greeted us, and Sarah instructed Flor to lie down on the table face down.

While I was listening to the conversation, I saw that the doctor was carefully observing the x-ray. "I'll check your back," he announced. The doctor approached the stretcher. He palpated the area of her dorsal vertebrae and counted them. "Turn left, please." He made her bend in a fetal position, then back. "Lie on your back. With your legs close to your chest, turn to one side and the other. Now sit on the edge of the stretcher." He checked her reflexes and said, "Okay," while sitting next to the desk and opening a document in his computer he added, "Please answer this questionnaire in the most honest way possible."

While Flor was on the computer, I tried, "Doctor, how are the results of the x-ray?"

"I would prefer to answer when your daughter can also listen in a couple of more minutes." He continued writing on his papers. I looked at Sarah. She, like an accomplice, winks at me. Her smile was a balm for my heart. Flor finished, and the doctor asked Sarah to print the answers.

With all the information in his hands, and in a very professional way, he explained, "Well, according to the x-ray, the curve increased in the last three months from 35 to 55 degrees. It is significant. If the curvature was greater on the top of the spine, I would say that the operation is urgent since it affects the thoracic capacity and often causes heart problems. In Florence's case, the steepest curve is the lower spine. That curve does not affect other organs. However, you should know that the curve will continue to advance over the years. Although progress is very slow, the greatest impact is experienced in general in old age. The operation is not urgent, not life or death. There are people who never have an operation. But if we consider the result of the psychological test, I can perceive that this curvature is significantly affecting Florencia's self-esteem at her fifteenth birthday.

Considering all the factors and given all the characteristics of the case, I would be willing to operate. But I want you to know that the decision is yours."

A fierce storm broke out in our lives. Flor's father refused permission for the operation to proceed. I was afraid, but more afraid of Flor's daily suffering. Eli was, as always, my rock. As a couple, we considered all the possible outcomes and consequences, the darkest and the brightest scenarios. Whatever I decided, he would support me. Then began the wait, the tests and follow-up telephone discussions with her father. Flor was active in a scoliosis forum and felt supported. She saw the sun in the midst of the storm in her soul. As my disagreement with her dad was growing, she often thought of herself as a rope pulled from both ends. As the days passed and the opinions distanced, the rope tensed more and more, and seemed ready to break. Flor was distressed, but sure. She would undergo the operation despite not having the consent of her father. If I had to sign a document taking full responsibility for the outcome, I would do it.

The Unexpected

We arrived at the hospital at six o'clock in the morning: Eli, Rebecca, Flor and me. Her father, who changed his mind and came from Argentina, was there, as were my parents, who had come from

Uruguay and stayed at our house. Everyone seemed scared. The nurses connected electrodes all over her body and poked an IV in her arm. They measured blood pressure, temperature and left us waiting. They would come looking for Flor when the operating room was ready. The fear was disguised among nervous jokes. After a long wait, the doctor appeared dressed in his surgery gown and gave us the news. "I regret to inform you that the surgery was canceled. An emergency case arrived and there is no room available."

"And now?" I stammered as Flor's gaze fell on the doctor's eyes.

"Now we have to coordinate again. We depend on the anesthetist, the operating room availability, me and the other technicians who assist me. In the summer it's more difficult because there are fewer operating rooms available. Give me a couple of days to see what the first date will be that we can get. Don't expect it to be any sooner than two to three months from now."

"Two or three months?" repeated the indignant father. "I came especially from Argentina! It's not around the corner."

"I understand and believe me I did everything possible to be able to operate today knowing that you were here. But I couldn't do anything. I am so sorry. Sarah will come in a few moments to discharge you

Say YES, Ask questions later

for today and I promise to communicate with you as soon as possible with the new date."

We remained silent. Flor couldn't stop crying and I hugged her tightly. Why her? Why so much suffering? What would she do now? How would I support her? I felt for her dad. And my parents, what would they say? How long would it take until they gave us a date? How much would it take for Flor to prepare emotionally for this?

"Hang in there Mariana, you have to be strong and calm for Flor," I repeated as a mantra to myself. Her father was giving Flor a hard hand squeezing. Eli hugged Rebecca. We were all united by solidarity and silent crying.

"What do you want to do, mi amor?" I asked.

"Sleep and not wake up until the day of surgery. I cannot think anymore. I'm very tired, ma."

It broke my heart. I was devastated. I didn't know how to comfort her. I don't know where her dad got energy to take Flor on a trip. I appreciated his positive attitude and felt very grateful for it. I had been paralyzed. We were all exhausted. My parents couldn't get over their astonishment. The experience was unknown to them as in South America medicine was private. This was incomprehensible for them.

Two days later, Sarah called. She gave us the new date. Another month and a half to wait. She would not be there that day and that worried me. When she was there, everything was easier. She calmed me down and promised to talk to the person who would be in her place to take care of Flor and me. I trusted her. This time we would plan it differently. In order to prevent the troubles of another last-minute cancelation. My parents would not travel, and her dad would be notified by me once Flor entered the operating room only then he would take the flight. He would arrive the next morning, when his daughter would be recovering.

And like all things, the day arrived. We were back at 6 a.m. in the hospital. This time it was just Flor, Eli and me. Again, the procedure as before: the electrodes, the IV, the pressure, the temperature and wait.

"The time has come. Are you ready?" The nurse asked.

"Yes, super ready," Flor said in a confident voice.

"Can I accompany her?" I asked.

"Of course!"

Eli whispered something in Flor's ear, kissed her, and then said to me, "I will be waiting for you in the cafeteria."

Flor was on a stretcher the nurse was pushing. We walked through long and endless corridors. I did not let go of her hand. She held onto mine, strong, without saying a word. The nurse complained about the elevators. I don't remember what she said. We entered the operating room. A room full of spotlights that came from all directions. Many devices. The doctor greeted us. I don't remember much more. I released Flor's hand for an instant, so they could move her over to the operating table.

Once more, Flor and I looked at each other and smiled. Hands clasped, intertwined more strongly than ever.

"Now we are going to inject a white liquid. It is anesthesia. It won't hurt. It will put you to sleep right away," said the technician.

Flor was staring at me. "I love you, mi amor," I said. And while she tried to answer me with a smile, she fell asleep. Her fragility and mine became one. They gave me her shoes, and in that moment, I realized that I had handed my daughter's fate over into the hands of the surgeon and the universe. Everything could change forever.

I couldn't contain myself; as I left the operating room, I cried inconsolably. The nurse hugged me and reassured me, "It's normal, you were strong for your daughter. Now that she doesn't see you, you can cry quietly. That's how we moms are."

I found Eli in the cafeteria. He had fallen asleep. It was hard to stop crying. I tried to calm down to call her father. "Flor is in the operating room. Everything is alright. You can board the flight. I'll send you a message as soon as she is out. It might take more or less seven hours. That's what they told us. She went in fifteen minutes ago. Have a nice trip. Chau."

Eli woke up. "All right? Why do you cry, love? Everything will be fine. Come, Marika, calm down."

Those were the longest, hardest hours of my life. As Sarah promised, the nurse informed me every so often, "She reacted well to anesthesia; the screws have been placed; they are about to end; everything went as expected; now she's in the recovery room."

Every time she let me know something, it helped me get through the endless hours. Now I needed to see her, stroke her hair, hold her hand. I knew that difficult times were coming, but I didn't care. It had been eight hours when the doors opened, and the stretcher came out. Flor had her eyes open. She looked at me, smiled at me and, while a tear rolled down her cheek, she said, "Ma, I'm straight! Thank you!"

I deeply admired this strong and determined girl. With one of her eyes closing due to fatigue and the effects of anesthesia, my daughter added, "Can you give me my cell phone?" I exploded in a laugh. How could she think of the cell phone? Life went on and those hours when the watch had stopped were already over. Her happiness was greater than the pain she felt between painkillers. Her desire to recover exceeded the expectations of the doctor.

She woke up with her father present, stroking her hair. "Daddy! You arrived!" She was radiant.

I helped her put on her pajamas with drawings of cupcakes and I made two braids with her long hair.

Say YES, Ask questions later

She asked to sit on a chair. Later she climbed some stairs accompanied by the physiotherapist. In the afternoon the doctor came. He was extremely happy with the results. He called Flor the poster girl. The next day she was discharged. Everything seemed like a dream! It was an encouraging week watching Flor regain her joy.

What Else Could Happen?

It was Friday and we were preparing breakfast.

"Ma, can you change my gauze, my dad is coming to pick me up in half an hour?"

"Of course, mi *amor*."

"How does the scar look?"

"On the top looks great. On the bottom of the scar is red and a yellowish liquid is still coming out. Let me smell the gauze." Worried, I called Eli. "Eli! Could you come for a moment?"

"Don't show me the wound. You know I get woozy easily," he confessed when he approached.

"Can you smell this?"

"It smells very ugly, like rotten," he said.

I called the doctor. When her father arrived, we all left for the hospital. The doctor decided to do a swab to rule out infection. We spent the weekend nervous, waiting for the results of the test the doctor did. It was nine o'clock on Monday morning. I went to work to distract myself a little when the phone rang at the store.

"Yes, I'm Flor's mom. No! I can't believe it! And what can be done? Is this necessary? I understand. No, she didn't eat anything. She is still sleeping. Okay. We'll be there in half an hour. I hung up and called Eli. "Wake Flor up and don't let her eat anything. We have to go to the hospital as soon as possible. I will explain as soon as I get there. I'm leaving now." I got in the car. The phone rang again. It was Flor.

"Why are you crying, my little girl? Don't be afraid, it's going to be alright. I will arrive in two minutes. Tell your dad to meet us at the hospital."

In the car I explained to Flor and Eli. Upon arrival we met her father and proceeded again to Admission. They announced us and in a few minutes Dr. Moreau arrived. He told us that they had found staph infection. It could be very problematic because it is close to the medulla, and this was a delicate area. They needed to prepare her for a surgery to perform some clean-up and then continue with antibiotics for safety.

Her dad asked, "Can it be treated with antibiotics and see what happens?"

"I will do what you tell me; but if it were my daughter, I would not risk it. An infection in the spinal cord can be lethal," the doctor warned. There was nothing more to discuss. It was time to move forward.

"Tomorrow I must travel to a convention, but I will not leave without first operating on Flor. Please bear

Say YES, Ask questions later

with me. I don't know what time I can get a free operating room. Flor, meanwhile, you must keep fasting. Be patient."

Everything was confusing. Just when we thought the nightmare was over, we felt that it had just begun. It was a very long day, full of uncertainty and fear. At ten-thirty in the evening the nurse came to take her. She left with her dad. I do not know if I was in surrender or in shock.

This time I didn't shed tears. This time it was Eli who cried inconsolably. The only thing he said between sobs was, "Why? Why she, who was so brave?"

This time the wait was shorter, two hours instead of eight. Everything in life is relative. Flor came out of the surgery sad, sore and starving. This time she had staples instead of stitches. This time she was not the poster girl. She was a frightened little girl, tired and feeling pain burning from within. This time it would be a month in the hospital. The suffering, the nights listening to suffering from other children, the veins that did not cooperate, the comings and goings in the middle of the night, the solidarity of the nurses, was a world foreign to us that became our new reality. Everything is relative. Thirty days of maximum alert as we said "No. That medicine constipates her. No, that physiotherapy, no. They can't find her vein. No..."

Thirty days of falling in love with Paris, the always happy eight-month-old baby despite the fact her mom couldn't be there to cuddle her. Everything is relative.

One night, at three o'clock in the morning, we woke up to the cries of the girl who shared the room with Flor. She writhed in pain and her mother didn't know what to do; the mother told us this had been happening every day for the last five years. It was heartbreaking. We couldn't handle it anymore. At four in the morning I requested a discharge under my responsibility. Flor had exhausted her body and soul. Me? I don't even know. I operated on autopilot in those days. So, Eli took us home.

The recovery was slow and painful. In September Flor re-started high school. She would fall asleep sitting in class. Her body was not responding. The effects of two anesthesia and two surgeries took a toll on her. The first academic exams arrived. They didn't reflect Flor's efforts. The winter made her recovery extremely difficult. We requested a meeting with the High School principal, a wise man and very loved by his students. He advised her, "Leave the semester and listen to your body, which clearly is asking for rest. You are an excellent student. There is no need to lower your averages. These grades are not reflecting the student you truly are although these are the ones that will be considered when you enter university. Don't punish yourself! By hurrying you won't always come out ahead."

Say YES, Ask questions later

Flor listened attentively. It took her a few weeks to accept that her body couldn't stand it anymore. She left the semester and went to Uruguay to enjoy the summer with her extended family.

CHAPTER 10

Be Part of the Community

It was a super busy morning. I needed to order merchandise and make important calls. I asked Alice not to forward me any calls, so when she appeared with the phone in her hand and a face that said, "this call is important," I looked up at her.

"It's Holly, from the party, Des' mom," Alice said.

Holly called to tell me that one of the girls I met at that first party in her house had colon cancer. She told me that Keri was very young, not more than twenty years old. She invited me to be part of an event that they would organize to raise funds for treatment that Keri would need. She asked me if I wanted to sell there and donate a percentage of sales.

I joined the project immediately. Now I could help others while working. "Work and help. Be a part of it," I repeated again. I saw it clearly! This was the *why* I searched for over so many years. This was my purpose! It was not the money or my career, not a new car, not the biggest house. Suddenly I discovered a world of different people, with different values, and I saw things clearly.

It was like the day the eye doctor gave me a pair of glasses to see from afar. I went outside, and I couldn't believe it. I read all the posters that I had previously

Say YES, Ask questions later

only recognized from their shapes or colors. Now I could distinguish the details. How had I not realized I did not see? It was hard to stop thinking and focus on the orders and calls I had on my list for the morning,

It was already after 6 p.m. in the evening. We had closed the door and turned off all the lights. Alice and I were struggling to find an error that would not let us finish the cash balance.

We saw a car approaching the parking lot. A lady came down and stuck her nose against the window. Immediately I left what I was doing, opened the door, turned on all the lights and invited the woman to come in. Her name was Shirley, and she couldn't conceal her amazement, just as she couldn't stop expressing her thanks, "How kind, thank you very much! I came from the other end of the city and I got lost on the road, that's why I arrived late. Please, excuse me! Soon it will be my birthday," she continued, and a friend told me that I could celebrate here. Is it true that you have a space for our get-togethers? She also told me that you could teach us how to wear scarves. Is that right?"

"Yes. That's right," I answered, and invited her to go upstairs to the events space.

It was big and private. There was a small kitchen where the hostess could prepare coffee and serve some snacks. There were chairs for about twenty people and a couple of tables available if needed.

Shirley asked me for the cost of renting the space.

"Nothing!" I replied. I was grateful that she brought friends to the store who didn't know of our existence. How could I charge her?

I explained I could share some tips on how to use the shawls and it would take me about fifteen or twenty minutes, depending on the interests of the group. We went ahead and booked the date and time for her event. She was very happy. In appreciation, that same night she bought a wallet and a scarf that I saw her use years later with special affection.

Shirley invited more than forty people to her birthday because usually, only half attended. That afternoon thirty-five arrived. Eli ran to buy more chairs to accommodate all the guests. Again, the women couldn't believe that behind that small door they entered, they would discover a magical world of colors, accessories and trips to distant lands they didn't know were hidden there.

After an hour of wandering through the corners of the store trying to choose purses, assemble sets or fight over the last pieces of Israeli silver, we invited them to go upstairs to the space where Shirley offered them drinks and snacks. Then we gave each a scarf and a clip and explained the different ways to use them.

"Hello, I'm Mariana. In Edmonton they know me as the scarf lady with an accent," I told them, alluding to my English with strong Latin rhythm. "Actually, I do not know why they call me that." The women laughed shyly. I told them in a few words my love story and how the business started. I shared the interest shown by so many ladies throughout the years since I had arrived in Canada, pondering my scarves and the different ways to use them. I proceeded to teach how to tie the scarves.

"Take the scarf and place it in front of you," I indicated while waiting for them to imitate me. "Choke yourself," I said with my strong accent. The women exploded with laughter. "Please, don't do this in front of angry husbands or grumpy coworkers. It can be dangerous as they might like the idea...Now unchoke, put your hands in front and move your right palm saying 'Hola!'"

And so, at Shirley's birthday party, I started, without realizing it, giving workshops on the use of accessories. The women adored these moments of play and laughter where they acted like little girls playing dress up again. Princess Florence became the playground for adult girls. The more I did it, my self-confidence grew until I was daring to offer a variety of fashion related workshops throughout the province. I understood that my personal story was more relevant to them than what they learned about accessories. My story conveyed hope. It was a story of love, effort and success.

My God, this is Paradise!

Catherine was short and bubbly. Her beguiling smile and spectacular shoes with towering heels helped her look taller than she was. Through the years I learned that her heart was much bigger than the small body that contained it. I met her at a networking event and exchanged cards. One day she called me on the phone. I appreciated her taking the initiative. "Are you going to stay late today? I want to visit the store and chat with you," she said.

"I will wait for you!" I saw her enter the premises and look surprised. I watched her from the mezzanine. She didn't see me. Her big eyes, her mouth open in wonder, and the already common response, "My God, this is paradise!"

I relished every time a new client came in the store and pronounced those words. Some also added sighs or little jumps which gave a funny touch to the scene. They all looked like girls entering a candy store. I was delighted to watch Catherine jumping in her black and white zebra-like high heels. I went down to welcome her and invited her to come upstairs to the events room that served as my office during the day.

Her eyes didn't know where to look first. "How can it be that I never heard of you?" she asked. "Your prices are fantastic, very reasonable, and you have beautiful things. I have to call my friends. No, we better talk first; I want to know all about you, so I can connect you better with the right people." She listened intently to my story. She was entertained, and I could see her enjoying it. Then it was her turn. I was curious to know what motivated her to connect with me. She shared about her computer company, her plans and her volunteering in Suit Yourself, one of the many organizations she is a part of.

"Tell me more; I'm interested," I said.

"Suit Yourself is a non-profit organization dedicated to providing formal clothing to women who return to the workplace after traumatic experiences such as abusive marriages, drugs or alcohol. We provide clothing to low-income immigrant women as well. According to the type of work they acquire, we give them two or three sets of clothes, free of charge. This might include capes, shoes, purses and accessories.

The organization is maintained with clothing donations and with the proceeds from a high tea once a year. There are different ways to collaborate, in addition to the entrance ticket. For example, this year four teams were created, each led by a woman of influence in our community. Each team presents two models for a fashion show at the high tea, where more than five hundred women attend. These teams also compete to get as many monetary donations two or three months before the event. I am the captain of one of the teams and I would like to invite you to join us. I thought if you could donate some accessories for our models it would be fabulous and will give you a lot of exposure at the high tea."

"Count on it, for sure. Let them know they can come and find what they need. But I would like to help even more. Hmm ... let me think. I know! In two weeks, we have plans for an Argentine Sunday at the store. Many people will attend because it's free and also super fun. I have hired tango dancers who will teach my clients how to dance and we will serve delicious empanadas with Argentine wines. I think we could ask for donations of clothes and sell them at the event. Also, I can donate a percentage of that day's sales to Suit Yourself if you will also help me promote it. What do you think?"

"Too generous on your part; so much is not necessary. I'm going to promote you, regardless of everything. Your business is spectacular, and it has to stop being Edmonton's best kept secret."

"Thanks! I want to be part of this wonderful work you are doing. Do not forget that I am also an immigrant and that touches me closely."

"Well then welcome to our Panache team. It's a pleasure to have you with us. You are going to meet some amazing women."

Catherine was right! In the team there were lawyers, a Wall Street etiquette consultant, and many other well-known entrepreneurs in the community. It was an impressive experience to see these women roll up their sleeves and get to work sorting, ironing and organizing the clothes their friends donated. The clothes were incredible: famous brand outfits, shoes never worn, like-new formal dresses. The day of the high tea, it was wonderful to gaze at those women dressed in high heels and sophisticated hats, recreating English royalty. There were silent auctions, raffles and popular branded handbags were sold. The best prize was a whole year of free shoes from the best shoe stores in the city.

"Next year," I thought, "it will be a whole year of Princess Florence accessories." So, it was. In the next edition of the event, in addition to donating the big prize consisting of accessories for the whole year, I gifted each of the five hundred women in attendance, a cute mini-coin purse. People loved it! As a sponsor I had the opportunity to share my story and a short version of my scarf demo.

Doors began to open before me in a magical way. It was during that event I met Dianna, a woman who touched my heart in a special way.

Fabulous at 50

Dianna Bowes was the director of Fabulous at Fifty, an organization that promoted trade shows and activities for fifty-year-old ladies. I introduced myself. I liked the serenity she transmitted. She was the living image of a healthy, active woman, enjoying life at fifty. For a sedentary person like me, no doubt, she was a role model. I became part of her annual trade show and over time, we built a beautiful relationship.

I started to join her for walks where we would exchange ideas and come up with new projects. Together we attended countless workshops, music festivals, and all kinds of fun activities. We took a trip to Uruguay and Argentina, where we had a great time discovering a different way of living, which she loved! It was fun to see my country and things that were familiar to me through her fresh eyes. That gave me perspective and helped me recognize the skills I acquired there without even knowing. She was an excellent observer and saw things I never saw before. She was the perfect travel companion, always ready, always happy for a new adventure. After that trip, we had planned many more trips to go together. But life got in the way; her life was cut short at the young age of sixty-one, when an aggressive cancer took her without compassion. Her wise words never stopped popping up in my head, "If not now, when?" As I write I cry, because it still feels unreal; she is not here anymore to text or ask her a silly question just to hear her calming voice.

I learned from her to live in the present moment to the fullest as she did, to put things in perspective, to see the best in every person we met, and to appreciate the smallest things in nature. She was a survivor of an inhospitable world and had a history full of silences and abandonments. She was given up in adoption at birth to her grandparents. Growing up in a turbulent home where fights and alcohol issues were common every day, she learned to become invisible to avoid being the target of the turmoil. At a very young age, she married her high school sweetheart and began the life she dreamed of.

Despite her difficult background, she saw life in multi-color. Dianna inspired me in a way that made me want to emulate her and reach my fifties also in multi-color. What that meant was I started doing exercises and eating healthy food. I learned to rest, to give myself time, book dates for a massage, or a manicure without guilt. Dianna taught me that caring for myself wasn't about being skinny or pretty, it was to accept myself as I was. "You need to take care of the body that would hold and contain your soul for the following fifty years," she would say kindly but firmly. "That is the only way possible you could experience the future with joy, strength, continue traveling, being independent, and becoming a fun grandmother." Her wisdom will stay with me forever.

Through Dianna, I met a world full of solidarity and women united by a clear slogan: to help each other grow, to have fun, to love, be loved while taking care of ourselves. Therefore, my life was filled with new people, people who lived life in a way I had always dreamed of: giving, sharing experiences, and helping others. This was a multi-colored life, living

Mariana Konsolos

without fear of letting go or expecting anything in return. I was an active member and, at times, a co-leader of that community of diverse and wonderful women growing and flourishing, reaching new peaks of splendor unknown to me. I was discovering, hallucinating the best version of myself, and I loved every minute of it! I learned to recognize the extraordinary feeling of being able to share life's lessons learned without care about being judged.

To give for the pleasure of giving—this gave me a sense of fulfillment very difficult to explain to someone who was raised in the same community as I was in Uruguay. I became aware of all I learned at home and school through thirteen years of a military government in Uruguay that had left deep and defining scars. They taught us to live life in fear, distrust, and fear of judgment.

Sentences like these were not uncommon to hear back then: "Do not share your ideas; people will copy you. What will they think about you if you do that? Do not believe everything they say. They are bragging. People might want something from you. Be careful! Do not talk to strangers."

Suddenly I understood my rebellion and resistance all those years. I understood the lack of belonging I felt and suffered for so long. I did not want to live like that any longer. Everything I wanted and believed was judged as unacceptable in Uruguay. In Canada, all was welcomed and out in the open. I finally felt at home!

Self Esteem Doesn't Come in a Bottle

I walked into the vendors' meet and greet for the Fabulous@50 Trade Show. I felt intimidated as I didn't know a single person in the room. It seemed like most of the ladies knew each other from previous shows.

Kelly welcomed me at the reception. I knew about her but never met her in person. I admit the scars on her face, arms and legs got my attention.

Throughout the entire meeting, I observed her with admiration; she was moving around with confidence and grace. I felt an overwhelming desire to connect with her, learn, and discover the secret to her confidence, something I struggled with all my life.

Dianna took the stage. She shared her vision of the upcoming tradeshow and encouraged us to promote the event in our inner circles to make it a success for all. I was in!

Later we had time to network. I had the opportunity to connect with many entrepreneurs from the city, but my focus was to meet Kelly. I made sure to introduce myself. We chatted for a bit when she told me about a book she was about to publish. Immediately I offered to be one of her sponsors. That was the beginning of our long-lasting relationship and a true inspiration to my life.

I read her books and learned some of the details she went through after getting burned on seventy-five percent of her body when she was two years old. She was a living miracle, and her story hit right on my self-esteem button.

"People look at you for what, maybe thirty seconds?" she would say. "And then? They go back to themselves, to make sure their hair looks good or their extra kilo doesn't show through the shirt. Everybody is NAVEL-GAZING!"

I admit I needed to go to the dictionary to understand what that expression meant.

She continued, "Are you going to limit your life for those thirty seconds of judgment from someone you might never see again in your life? NO! Please don't give them the power of your life!"

That took me to my teen years when I wouldn't go to the beach because I was fat. I laughed at myself. Who would remember I wasn't there? NOBODY! Only me, and it was my loss.

One day, she shared a post on Facebook, stating she was lucky not to have hair on her chin to pluck as it was skin graft from her belly. I found that hilarious! Her sense of humor was refreshing. She knew how to turn drama into comedy, and that was a lesson I needed badly. I was taking life so seriously, being hard on myself. I needed to loosen up.

Say YES, Ask questions later

Over the next few years, we became closer and closer; we shared hardships and happy times. I learned from Kelly not to deny feeling fear. Feeling scared to divorce with three kids didn't prevent her from doing it. Overcoming the fear and taking full responsibility was her way of living. Until today it is inspiring to watch her choosing to live life on her own terms—not to be a victim, but the character in charge of her own story. Her loyalty and determination to her own values are definitely her biggest lessons in the world.

CHAPTER 11

On Top of the Mountain

2013 was a year of great changes and major achievements. Flor finished high school and was accepted to several universities. They were all far away and I regretted having to separate from her because I enjoyed her company and her understanding of the world around her. We took a beautiful trip together to visit the universities and so that she could choose where to settle down for the next four years. I was very excited to be able to share this quest with her. It was hard for me to think about the idea of her leaving home, but I totally understood her. I was once an eighteen-year-old desperate for freedom and independence.

When I was seventeen, young and idealistic, wanting to change the world. I was different from my friends at school. I was not interested in clothes or outings. I was bored with gossip and topics without substance. I got along with a very diverse crowd. Listening to their stories my life was enriched. I had younger and older friends, poorer and richer friends, some more educated and some uneducated. Each one of them were sources of information I had no access to otherwise.

Say YES, Ask questions later

Seen as an outsider by friends and family I made the decision to travel to Israel with three friends from the youth organization I belonged to.

"Aren't you afraid to go with three guys?" asked the girls in my class, as they whispered among themselves.

"Afraid?" I replied incredulously. "Afraid of what?" In general, I didn't feel afraid, but going with three guy friends made me feel very protected. What's more, I felt like a princess. So, with an open mind and craving to know the world, I left behind a narrow-minded Uruguay. I left the Uruguay of fears embedded in the people since the military dictatorship of 1973, the Uruguay where nothing was questioned, and opinions had no place. I left a slow, mediocre and lethargic Uruguay.

I arrived in a very intense fast paced country, very opposite from everything I knew. In Israel, they struggled to survive, lived each day as if it was their last. I landed in a place where boys go to the army at eighteen and become adults overnight. But, in spite of everything, freedom was breathed in every corner and stone of that small country.

For the first five months, we lived in a kibbutz, a socialist community based on agriculture, in the north of the country. There they gave us a house and food in exchange for work. We all lived together, which was not easy I must admit. The disorder, the smells, the snoring and many other things, which I am embarrassed to share, were reasons for fights, complicity, but also for laughter. We managed to live together without major upheavals.

I worked in jobs doing tasks I had never done in my previous life as a South American Jewish princess. I spent some time in the community kitchen, where I washed dishes and served tables. I also cleaned the chicken coop, cleaned toilets, milked cows and looked after children. We woke up early and worked hard during the day. We became friends with a group from England who were volunteering in the harvesting of oranges. They drank a lot and were often drunk. They spent afternoons lying in the sun chatting, laughing with us and doing nothing. It was all new to me. In Uruguay we didn't drink at all; we were so naive!

The second five months we moved to an institute for international leaders in Jerusalem. There we met people from all over the world. While we had many things in common, we were also very different. I remember Mariana and Sandy, two Mexican girls with whom I was curiously imagining how freedom steered their lives. I also met a group of young people from my country who came from a Uruguay that I didn't know. They came from an unprivileged Uruguay, with real needs and without luxuries. They introduced me to a Uruguay of sacrifice and solidarity.

Say YES, Ask questions later

I learned about politics, about religion and its extremes. I learned about the differences between being Sephardic and Ashkenazi. I lived it. But what impressed me most were the Israeli guys. They lived a very peculiar reality. My friends and I had graduated from high school and soon we would go to university, but they would go to the Army. What scared us to the death they were looking forward to. They considered serving in risky roles exciting and thrilling. They wanted to enroll to be pilots and paratroopers. We would consider administrative jobs better considering they were safe. They laughed at our fears and how they ruled our lives, while they, without perceiving it, were dominated by an exacerbated patriotism.

I didn't pay attention to Flor's needs and fears. I wanted to believe she had the same uncontrollable desires as I had as an eighteen-year-old becoming free. What I couldn't remember was the fear and needed love and support I craved from my parents. I left her alone with a freedom that generated fear and that she wasn't prepared to face. I didn't know how to accompany her, teach her to cook, to keep up with the household tasks. I thought that by giving her a place to live I was done. I didn't realize that I had given her an apartment full of things and emptiness. That was not what she needed. She only needed my love.

While she was trying to learn to fly on her own, I was distracted in my own flight. I was nominated for several prestigious awards: Distinguished Women of Edmonton, Women Entrepreneurs of Alberta, Latin Entrepreneurs. I was invited to give talks in different universities to students in Business School. I made presentations for immigrant entrepreneurs in NorQuest, the English school where I first met Elaine, my beloved teacher.

But while that was happening to me, Eli was staking his own claim that he was tired of the cold. His physique began to show signs of exhaustion from so many years of hard work. He wanted to enjoy life, and to travel the world.

He was beginning to think about retiring. I could not understand it. Why withdraw from something loved that's only growing bigger and better? One leaves a job you don't like, not one that fulfills you. But he didn't love the work he did. He worked because he had to. I understood that we came from different worlds. He learned from his family to work to survive, to cover the basic needs, and that conformism came with its own perk; they rest on weekends and have a safe income without many responsibilities. The joy came from things that were shared with family and friends. Work was to meet the immediate needs, that was it.

In my family, on the other hand, the emphasis was on the future, opportunities and possibilities to grow through education. They didn't know to stop to rest or enjoy themselves. They always worked. There was no place for free time. I heard my parents say they would die with their boots on, meaning, they would never retire. Eli was planning to retire at sixty as he had learned from his family, a thought that made me panic because that was about to happen in only two years for him, and I wasn't willing nor ready for retirement at fifty!

The Body

I was convinced that the business was ready to work without us being present. So that year we began to travel a month on and a month off. On one of those trips we went to Spain, a destination for which my soul had been yearning for years. Walking along the Costa Brava, on the edge of a cliff that joins two coves of spectacular nature, surrounded by lush vegetation and a transparent blue sea, Eli proposed that we sell everything in Canada and come live here. Who wouldn't have accepted the idea? A place where they speak my language, with this wonderful man and this natural paradise? It was a fantasy or maybe an incredible dream. I said YES, without much awareness of what my decision implied.

From that trip I also remember our visit to Granada. I was so overweight that the climb to the Alhambra was a nightmare. I close my eyes now and I see Eli pushing me from behind, while I'm running out of breath and sweating unbearably. I left my body unattended for many years and was paying the consequences. I had to make a drastic change. I could not continue like this. I had the time, the money, and this man to travel the world, but my body was not in tune. It was absurd not to have the health to enjoy it, so when I returned from my trip, I put together my action plan. I traded my morning coffee at Starbucks for a personal trainer. I eliminated the Facebook time at nights before I went to sleep, to get up an hour earlier to exercise. Knowing myself, I set up my training for 6 a.m. so I would be half asleep and have no time to talk myself out of it before Kevin, my trainer, would arrive.

I replaced the café visits with friends for walks with them. Meals were organized. I left behind the chocolates that, I thought, calmed my anxiety. Truth was, they gave me more anxiety. It was hard. There were days when I wanted to reject the discipline; my mind wanted to cheat convincing me that one day without training was okay. But that image in Granada was strong enough in my mind to push me to wake up because I didn't want to be that Mariana anymore.

The weeks and months passed, and I was getting more and more fit and happier every day. I regained the agility and energy that made me more youthful and dynamic.

My body began to be in harmony with everything that was happening in my life. I took care of myself and I liked to see myself like that. I felt ready to travel the world with avid eyes and a fit body. On my next trip with Dianna I discovered the world of walking. I enjoyed it immensely because it allowed me to talk to local people and smell and touch everything with my own hands. I got to places which could only be reached with my feet and my soul.

The Soul

During a presentation I gave for immigrants, I met Susana. She left the job at the hospital where I had seen her with Flor years ago. Now she worked at the Alberta Parkinson's Association. I offered to do 'The Magic of Scarves' workshop with the ladies who were afflicted with that disease and who met regularly. She liked the idea very much and the next day she confirmed the date. It was November 25th.

That day I had my morning coffee looking at the snow piled on the garden table. The temperature was around 20 degrees below zero, but with the strong wind and the inhospitable climate, it felt colder. I wondered if some of the ladies would leave their homes with that kind of weather for a meeting at the Parkinson's Association. I sent a message to Susana.

Around 10 a.m. she replied yes, there were eight women confirmed. When I arrived, they were sitting in a circle.

While arranging the scarves, Lisa, a lady with advanced illness, played the piano and sang. Her weak and stooped body trembled. Her sweet and firm voice didn't correspond with that deteriorated body. The women watched me, curious, while Lisa sang. When she finished, one of them asked me, "What are we going to do today?"

"We are going to play with scarves, but first I would like to know a little bit about you."

"I am Lisa. I was a music teacher at the University until I got sick. I kept going for a while, but each time it was getting harder, so a few years ago I retired."

"I'm Mary, I was a bank manager and I worked until Parkinson's advanced so much that I could not dress alone. I stopped working and moved to an institution where I have permanent help."

"Hi, I'm Helen. My husband has had Parkinson's for four years. The day he was diagnosed with the disease, I stopped working to help him."

And the women continued. One by one, they told me how wonderful their lives had been until Parkinson's arrived. Then it was my turn. "Well, I am Mariana, better known as 'the scarf lady with an accent." They laughed. Then I told them that I arrived in Canada fifteen years ago, where I met my current husband. I omitted how we met, fearful of their

Say YES, Ask questions later

judgment as they were an older crowd. I explained that in Uruguay I owned a real estate agency, a children's clothing store and a construction company and despite I was well off financially, I wasn't happy.

I continued my story, "In Canada nobody recognized my experience because I could hardly speak. My English was basic. I felt as if they put all my knowledge into a bottle with a very small opening. It felt as if I had no voice. My voice was perceived like a twelve-year-old child: little vocabulary, poorly armed phrases, misspellings when I had to connect in writing. Once I spoke, people would think that I surely did not have much education, that I had never read a book. It was very difficult to accept this new reality. I would never be the Mariana I had left behind in Uruguay. I could never learn in English the vocabulary I had acquired during thirty years of life in Spanish.

I got to the conclusion that I had two options: complain or do something. Suddenly I remembered the thousands of things I always wanted to do and for which I never had time while working like a maniac in Uruguay. I used to tell myself, "When I have time I will paint, I will knit. When I have time, I will go to ..." The list was very long! I turned my body and waved my hand, saying, "So, one morning I got up, looked back and said goodbye to the Mariana I was when I lived in Uruguay. That Mariana stayed there. I was in Canada now and I was a new Mariana full of opportunities and time. I slowly began to paint, knit and do a lot of things that I had been postponing for years. I even looked after children, who I always loved."

Suddenly Mary stopped me and said, "You're telling my story!"

"Nnn...no. It's...it's mine," I stammered, confused.

"Don't you realize? None of us could say goodbye to the person we were before our illness. It's so true what you say! How come I didn't see it before? I always wanted to be part of a choir, and I don't know why I'm not pursuing that now that I have time. I always wanted to have more free time to read and now that I have the time I am not reading!"

A chill ran down my body. Susana looked at me petrified. At that moment I understood the immensely therapeutic power of my story. These women were able to project themselves because I didn't talk about the disease they suffered with. I talked about love and my suffering as an immigrant. For a moment they were able to forget their suffering to empathize with mine. They could be in accord with the solution I had chosen. Suddenly they realized that my solution also served them.

Say YES, Ask questions later

Christmas Party at Princess Florence

As another year drew to a close, it was time for our Christmas party. The inspiration this time was the carnival of Venice, Italy.

"This year will be a special party," I thought happily. It was well deserved by the team who worked almost alone, the clients who supported us unconditionally, and us. It had been an incredible year and we had to celebrate our great achievements and infinite blessings. At the Latin gala I met Andrea Pinna, an Italian gentleman. When I heard him sing it seemed that I was listening to Pavarotti. My skin bristled, and my heart smiled overflowing with emotion.

Immediately I knew I had to hire him because he represented the spirit of the great celebration. He represented total passion, dedication and humility. This time we would present a fashion show, since we had imported a spectacular collection of Italian clothes. The models would be our own clients: real women, of all shapes, sizes and colors. There were housewives, teachers, cleaners, nurses, hairdressers, administrative staff and lawyers. There would be young ones and seniors, ladies of the church, retired women, married girls and single women.

Each one represented one of the many sectors of the community we served who loyally were following us. Eli decided on the menu; he would prepare a traditional Italian dinner: antipasto, homemade lasagna and tiramisu. There were wines and chocolates. We would close with a delicious and fresh limoncello.

The weeks before the party were intense and fun. With the girls' help, we decorated the store with the colors of Italy. The Christmas tree was adorned with mini-purses. They were green, red and white. We created a beautiful display. We had Venetian masks everywhere and colored necklaces in every corner. On the top floor we set up a wall with balloons representing the Italian flag. We made the canals of Venice with shawls of infinite shades of blue and turquoise that formed the waves. You could feel the joy in the air. We were all very happy.

Then the great day arrived. Everything exceeded our expectations. More than one hundred and fifty people visited the store during that day. There were people who arrived at ten in the morning when we opened and didn't leave until seven in the evening. Among them Helen, the lady whose husband had Parkinson's, came with a friend. She greeted me, hugged me and whispered in my ear, "You don't know how you've changed my life."

It was a day full of emotions. I met a lot of dear people that were part of my story whom I had not seen for a while: the whole group of girls from the church, the girls of the sorority, my dear Holly, Tema and her mom, Dianna, and many people very close to my heart. It was an unforgettable day. When Andrea sang, I could feel his voice seeping into the soul of the audience. They listened with closed eyes, hiding some tears of emotion in their cheeks. From a corner, I watched with amazement what we had created.

Our clients helped each other choose colors and accessories as they felt at home. They played at dressing up as executives, travelers, or dressed for a night of opera. They dreamed of going to Milan, they had fun and they laughed. When the fashion show started, the energy kept growing. It is true that the clothes were beautiful, but the emotional stories that we shared and that united us with these women surpassed the beauty that our eyes could perceive.

They transformed everything into something magical and very special. Each woman represented a piece in the life of the new Mariana in Canada. They were all part of the almost mystical communion that had been created. I was definitely at the top of the mountain!

CHAPTER 12

Change of Directions

On December 31st we were in Punta del Este having lunch with my parents when Eli's phone rang. It was Natalie, our business broker. "How strange!" I thought. We weren't expecting a call from her. Perhaps she lacked some information or details to be able to publish our advertisement.

We were selling our business. Eli met with her shortly after our trip to Spain. She suggested a price that I did not accept, and what follows was the tenor of the conversation.

Natalie said that she would do what we told her to do but she thought the price that we were asking was a bit high. Also, she wanted to make the point that selling a business is not like selling a house. It takes a long time to find the right person, especially in a case like ours.

After all, we had a quite complex operation and an extensive inventory. We asked how much time she thought it might take.

"I think...one to two years," she replied.

In my mind I was reassured that I had two more years to complete the sale of my business while I still enjoyed it. My plan was to develop key employees as associates. They would grow, and I would become more independent, so I could travel with Eli around

Say YES, Ask questions later

the world. This way I would not have to part with my beloved business.

Eli moved their discussion out to the backyard, so he could talk calmly. They talked for a long time.

Natalie's call was making me nervous. Why did she need to talk to him for so long? If it was just a simple detail that she needed, it would not take so long!

He returned to the table with a big smile and with a happy voice said, "There is an offer very close to what we asked for. A Canadian couple wants to buy the business and take possession of it in March. In a little while she is going to send us an email. Let's look at it and you can decide."

My parents celebrated the good news with Eli, asking more questions. I was silent. My blood ran cold. It was not what I wanted, expected or what Natalie had predicted.

Even though this was unexpected, I agreed to negotiate the price and later we managed to reach an agreement, signing a sale option that in thirty days conditions would be removed. On March 15th they would take possession of my company.

I called Flor to tell her. I thought she would be happy. She had never been a big fan of my business because she felt that Princess Florence had stolen her mom from her. I was surprised by her reaction. She was not communicating any amazement. In a worried voice, she asked, "Why, ma, if you love your job so much? Is everything alright? And what are you going to do?"

I didn't know what to answer, because I didn't know what was happening inside me either. Although it was true that six months ago, on that cliff on the Costa Brava, I told Eli that yes, I would sell the store to live in Spain, now I wasn't so sure. I could not explain why I signed that document just a few hours earlier.

"I still have time to back out," I thought that night when I went to bed. I could not understand why I signed. There was a force, like a strong instinct, that told me it was what I had to do. I wanted to understand why selling filled me with fears.

In recent times I felt Eli was distant and I didn't want to lose him. He was already fulfilled and happy with what we had. He didn't need more, until he started talking about retiring. He wanted other things. He wanted to walk, enjoy nature, be with friends, share with family. The winter cold of Edmonton forced him to be inside and that made him desperate to escape. Any excuse was good enough to travel as long as there was sun when he arrived.

I understood it because I too did not need more than what we had. I just needed my job, because that's where I connected with incredible people and my job allowed me to contribute things to the community, filling my soul. There I felt full and in balance; a little work, a little travel, family, friends. I felt that we had the ideal life. I didn't see why it had to be changed. I struggled to understand why for Eli the time we spent traveling was not enough.

I felt that I had to choose again, but what worried me the more wasn't deciding. I began to panic thinking I could fall back into a depression like the one I had suffered previously. There was no price in the world worth paying for the emotional stability I had acquired in the last ten years.

I believe I signed because I fully trusted Eli. I knew that his decisions were prudent and thoughtful. His wisdom of life always gave me peace. What he couldn't predict from behind his stable and calm gaze was how deep the wound in me would sink. He couldn't imagine that the monsters would visit me again in the days and months to come, and that they would slowly take over my sad soul and shake the very foundations of my essence.

I was not good at hiding my feelings, at keeping secrets, and this secret in particular was one requiring a lot of effort. I tried to continue with my walks and enjoy sunsets by the beach. I wanted to be distracted so as not to think, not to feel. But slowly I sensed that my anger towards Eli was growing more and more, like a storm of thick clouds that were slowly forming. I did not understand why all this was happening. A few days ago, I was feeling on top of the world. We were well!

Now, I felt an earthquake deep inside aggressively shaking the foundations of the structure we created together. Everything made sense while we both wanted to work, raise our daughters, make progress, acquire assets and move forward. Together, we managed to build a strong and beautiful building. Now, instead of proceeding to inhabit it, we would leave it empty. We crossed the finish line, reaching our goals in record time. Instead of continuing to move that rolling train to the next mark, we were about to stop right there. That's it, that's all, that's enough! After this, is there nothing else? I felt I was falling into a void of nothing.

Save the Secret

When we returned to Canada, I wasn't the same person anymore. The spark in my eyes was gone. I did not feel like going to work. I felt like an imposter. I stopped going to events in the community because I didn't want people to notice my sadness. And the hard days began with the lawyers, the disagreements, and the discussions. There were days when I wasn't willing to compromise, as an attempt at an unexpressed boycott. Other days I gave in, because I wanted this torture I was living to end as soon as possible.

My friends provided a lot of emotional accompaniment for me during those difficult days, but the closest to my heart was Flor, my daughter. With a special wisdom and love, she took care of me from afar. She communicated daily, and I waited anxiously for her phone call, since that was the best half hour of my day. I enjoyed her stories, the news about her studies and her jokes.

Every week it seemed that the lawyers were less in agreement. The due date was postponed week by week and the wear became increasingly unbearable. The tension between Eli and me was growing by leaps and bounds. The anguish had taken over my body. Every day I felt more or less disconnected from the outside world. And what about Eli? He spoke to me and I heard him only in the distance, "My love, why can't you see it? This is an opportunity. You are being paid for what you built from scratch with your work and your heart. It is an immense recognition that not many people achieve in life. You have done it in ten years. You should be so proud!"

"I didn't do it for the money. You know well that I never thought about selling it."

"I know it's not because of the money. But you have to be realistic. The situation in the province is going to get complicated, a recession is coming, the price of oil is falling all over the world."

"Princess Florence doesn't depend on recessions or crisis. I'm not afraid of changes. On the contrary, those issues push me to improve, to create new things, to be better." I responded in anger and frustration. I was devastated. Our life journey hit a rut on the rough road, the cart jiggled, everything was unsettled.

"We're going to have time for long trips. Didn't you want to travel to India? We can go after all this is over."

"I don't want to go anywhere anymore." I couldn't look at the future.

That afternoon we called Natalie. Eli was getting angry, raising his voice. He was also beginning to feel exhausted. I had not participated in the negotiations for a long time. I was not interested. But that day, when he hung up the phone with Natalie, he said, "Okay Mariana. I gave them an ultimatum. We go on a trip to Turkey with your cousins and on the way back we sign. If they don't accept, that's it. I cannot handle this anymore. There are no more extensions, no more new clauses." It was difficult to make Eli angry, but the lawyers had succeeded.

And so, in May, we went to Turkey for ten days with my cousins and their partners. Eli organized a wonderful trip that helped us to get away from the tension and stress we were experiencing. We were in spectacular places. We went to Istanbul, where we enjoyed beautiful walks on the Bosphorus. We ate delicacies and we toured the spice market delighting in its colors, aromas and textures. We enjoyed the abundance of a thousand-year-old culture. We traced the streets of the neighborhood where Eli had grown up. We entered the building where he had once lived.

Say YES, Ask questions later

The gentleman who sold teas in the hollow under the staircase of the building invited all of us to pass through to that tiny space where we couldn't enter standing.

Eli told us that the doorman of the building lived there with his family of five. There they cooked, slept and washed in brass basins of water heated with a primus. To go to the bathroom, they had to go to a public one a few blocks up the street. Once a week they went to the hammam, the girls with their mom and the boys with their dad. That was where the real bath took place. They scratched you with a kind of net with foam to take out the 'macarons' (shell of mud and skin).

The day of the hammam was the best day of the week according to Eli. That day was a man's day. As a child, Eli went to the hammam with his dad, the two of them alone. After the bath they went to a little bar where they ate delicious mussels stuffed with rice and pine nuts. His dad had a beer, and he gave Eli a small glass, so Eli could try it and *start becoming a man*. Then they went through the fish market and the sweet store where they made the small purchase of the day. Eli was able to show us all those places that still exist today.

We flew to Cappadocia, where we stayed in a cave hotel inside the hollows of the strange mountains. The experience was incredible, it was like being in a fairy tale. In the morning, very early, we climbed into a hot air balloon and from high in the sky we watched a perfect sunrise, one that magically lights the world each day. There was a special peace in those fields, the unique geography of the place rested the mind and caressed the soul. They waited for us around the corner with flowers and champagne, and although I knew that the scene was an extreme cliché, I enjoyed it intensely, because that was what my heart so desperately needed.

We went up to the mountain where the poorest peasants went to look for fresh and pure water from the mountains. For this they had to stand in line and wait long hours for their turn to fill their bottles. With the kindness that characterizes the Turkish people, they invited us to try the pure water without waiting in line, always taking care of the guests as their number one priority. We went into a store where cheeses were sold. I was touched by the generosity and humility with which the craftsman who made them welcomed us. There were no cheeses or olives that he didn't insist that we taste. He was proud of his products. I enjoyed watching him tell Eli the story of each cheese, of each olive.

I didn't understand a word in Turkish, but the passion could be seen in his eyes, in his gestures. The music of his words explained everything. I saw myself in that peasant selling his cheeses. It made me sad to say goodbye to him and to the happy me.

CHAPTER 13

The Sale

When we returned to Canada the stress, only briefly postponed, was there to greet us upon our arrival. The days were rapidly approaching toward the closing date for the sale of our company.

Every night it crossed my mind what the scene would be like when I would have to tell Alice, Sharon and Marlene, our Nana, about the sale. This episode repeated itself in my mind, as I imagined the different outcomes. Would they be angry? Would they leave? Would they stay? What would they say?

I thought about my clients, the providers, the people in the hospitals and nursing homes, where they knew me and waited for me to return. I tried to stay positive by imagining how I would pass on as much information as possible to the couple who were buying the company, so that they could continue with sales and events and success.

I made a plan. I started to document all the processes that we had implemented. I introduced the buyers to all our suppliers, to the managers of all the places where they would interact with stakeholders in their new business. I loaned them one of our smartphones. They did not own one and we wanted them to familiarize themselves with the applications and programs with which we managed and remotely ran the business.

I gave my last presentation with such anguish and a melancholy that was difficult to hide. It hurt every time I was invited to an event and I knew I wouldn't be in front of this company anymore. I couldn't stand any of those days because it forced me to hide the truth. My heart squeezed and every time I was afraid of making a mistake and that the farce would be exposed. It all made me wonder how people living a life of lies survive.

On June 30th, all trading conditions were finally removed. We had to terminate all of our staff contracts and the new owners would hire them again. I decided to tell Alice first and privately. One afternoon after work we were upstairs, in the mezzanine, and I told her we had to talk. "Alice, for quite some time now Eli has been very tired and has been talking about retirement. Next year he turns sixty. You have not been with us full time and I alone can't handle all of this ... so ...we have sold Princess Florence."

Alice's eyes filled with tears.

"Are you sure, Mariana? This is your blood, your life. Are you going to be fine? I understand Eli is tired, the work was very hard physically. We have to understand and support him." She hugged me, and we cried together.

I cried inconsolably because only Alice could understand the pain that I felt. She understood because she felt it too. She had also given her heart and cultivated this dream with me. Despite the fact that for the past few years she had worked only on weekends with us, she loved the company and still felt it was her own. Only she could read between the lines that this was an immense act of love from me to Eli. In a whisper and very gently she told me, "I know, Mariana, this is not what you want. This is what Eli needs."

Eli wanted to tell Sharon. He was the closest to her and felt he would know how to explain it best. But the days were passing, and Eli could not find the right time to speak with her. Then one afternoon, we went to pick her up at a fair, and while she was sitting in the back of the car sending texts, Eli told her, "Sharon, we wanted to tell you that we decided to retire."

"How good! When?" She asked absently, still immersed in her phone.

"Well, actually, we wanted to tell you that we sold the company."

She raised her head and with a sarcastic tone answered, "I hope it was a good deal."

I was petrified. I looked in the rear-view mirror. Trying to hide her anger, she went back to her phone and stopped the chance for any more conversation.

On June 1, 2015, the meeting that so often played in my head over the last six interminable months finally took place. The staff arrived along with the new owners. I was sad and watched everything from the side of the room. The tension was high. The air itself seemed to cry. There was silence and Eli began to speak, "Well, we are all here together because we wanted to tell you that Mariana and I are very tired and have decided to retire."

I saw Marlene looking at Alice in bewilderment, hoping to find an answer. Her eyes filled up with tears. Sharon and Beverly (another of the Filipino women who worked with us) looked at each other. Eli continued, "We were lucky to find this lovely couple who fell in love with Princess Florence and are willing to continue the path we started almost ten years ago. They are younger, they are full of new ideas, new dreams and many energies to take this project even further. You are a very important part of the success of the company, so it would be of vital importance that you could accompany them in this new stage that begins in fifteen days."

Marlene cried, Alice too. The rest reacted calmly, without much emotion. I was emotional. I don't know how I managed not to cry. I was full of fears, of anguish and many doubts. I admired the tranquility with which each one accepted the future. I was wondering if they were aware what this change would mean to them. Was it my lack of humility that made me believe they would miss or long for our support? We had always been there when they needed us. A free day, a letter of recommendation, a pay advance, a house to sleep in, a meal, a shoulder to cry on. "Maybe all this had value for me and not for them," I thought.

Then came the formalities. The new owners introduced themselves, told everyone who they were, what their dreams were. All of this unfurled while I vanished among the colors of the scarves hanging from Juanita, the straw giraffe that had witnessed all our adventures.

The next day everything felt different. A rare mixture of unknown feelings and emotions filled my body. I had freed myself from keeping the secret. I was anguished by having to part with everything that had been my daily life for so long. I felt that it was impossible to part with the routine, the creativity, the colors and textures. Why did I have to leave it behind? How could I take everything with me?

Letting go of the persona I had become over the last few years was tearing me apart and blurring out my identity. The sale was a loss in my eyes, and it hurt in my body, in my heart and in my words. I saw that my self-esteem had collapsed like a house of cards. It scared me seeing the opposite process that Eli was experiencing. He looked liberated, lighter than ever, more relaxed than ever! Could this be a crossroads where we were choosing different directions? I felt that I had to return to a position of protecting my vulnerability in front of the world. I didn't want anyone to see my terrifying fear of the future. I found myself looking for the weapons I had abandoned years ago, and without realizing it, I went back to war. After that morning I would enter the store sober and distant.

The training began and as if I was in the army. I limited myself to imparting instructions. I taught codes and strategies. I became hard and calculating. I hid my compassion in some deep drawer of the muscle that kept me alive. I was efficient and cold, and I carried an imaginary weapon that I had hidden in the back pocket of my pants to protect me from any attack. Not that I was going to use it, but every time someone asked me how I felt, I put my hand in my back pocket and stroked it thinking, "Do not hurt me too much, otherwise I will have to hurt you." After a week I had managed to distance myself from everything except Flor. She was the oasis in the desert where I lived. I welcomed her calls even though I received them with anxiety. She was life itself.

In the mornings I entered the store and began to give orders and distribute tasks among the workers. "Good morning, Sharon. We need to prepare the truck for the university. Who do you want to help you? Gerardo or Bev? Please, I ask you to share out loud the whole process that you follow to load the truck. The new owners are going to be your shadows today, so they can learn what you do and why."

"Gerardo can help me."

"Great, Bev can serve the customers at the store front."

After saying this, Sharon raised her eyes. For the first time in weeks she looked directly at me. Unable to contain the anger and sadness that oppressed her, she shouted, "I hate you! You left me alone! You were my life insurance! I knew that if something happened to me or my family, I would always have you. Now what will I do? I'm more alone than ever! My dad just died, and now you," she cried. She cried hard, as only a woman with a truly torn heart can cry.

"How can we explain that we will never abandon the wonderful human being you are?" I hugged her tightly as I stroked her hair and said, "Sharon, you will always have our support. You are our Sharon, a generous soul, full of life and creativity, full of energy and enthusiasm. You are a cheerful fighter who gave us your heart and gave the best of yourself to everyone who knows you. We will always take care of you and protect you. Our relationship never depended or ever will depend on your work. It's a connection of hearts." I heard Sharon breathe a sigh of relief.

My soul felt relief as well, after so many weeks of being frozen. But quickly the cold returned to my body as the days passed, as the change of command with the new owners took place. Egos grew, and I continued to distance myself. Humility, pride, wisdom and ignorance mixed in a mythical and mysterious dance. A power struggle invaded the space with such intensity that it was difficult to breathe there. I felt drowned in the place where, not long ago, had been my paradise of colors. I wanted to flee as soon as possible, to run away and never return. I tried to leave behind all the acquired knowledge, all the information and the endless hours of research that allowed me to take my enterprise forward. I tried to teach them the path that had led me to success. I tried to explain to them what it was that guided me to where I was, the why, the how. But, in return, I saw empty stares.

They didn't understand what I was talking about. I felt judged. They thought they could do better. I accepted this, and eventually I stopped trying to give them what they weren't ready to receive. I understood that everyone had the right and the obligation to make their own experience, to have their own failures and their own successes. And no matter how much good intention I had trying to save them from some scrapes, I did not possess the radical truth for them. My truth worked for me and emanated from the deep interior of my being, values and the interesting lenses I had been wearing for many years. Princess Florence was the faithful projection of what I was, believed and envisioned. It was multi-colored, thriving and full of life, and it filled with fantasy any space that was occupied. It was the very center of a community of women that revolved around this source of nuances and tonalities, travel, fashion, learning and a lot of feminine energy.

That's what I saw through my peculiar glasses with the violet frame and catlike shape that brought me closer to the success that others so longed for. I was selling the business for a figure so high that I couldn't even believe it myself, but it didn't make me happy.

On July 15th the money was deposited into our bank account. I looked at the statement on my computer. I thought about how people who win the lottery must feel. I could imagine people celebrating, buying dream cars, desired homes, going on incredible vacations. I cried because I didn't crave any of that. All I wanted was to continue caressing hearts, just as we had caressed them with Princess Florence.

That day I understood clearly that fulfillment for me was not dependent on wealth. Only the single question that kept repeating incessantly in my head, "Now what?"

CONCLUSION

Why Tell My Story?

I feel like singing!

After six hard months dealing with the sale of my business, I'm on the plane to Barcelona, a destination I dreamed for over thirty years. Even though I am very tired, I get no luck trying to rest. My thoughts are so many and so unruly it feels like thousands of butterflies are having a party in my head. So many plans and ideas, so much desire to live!
I carry some melancholy in my heart as I say goodbye to important pieces of the 'puzzle' that was the Mariana I became during my years in Edmonton.

Slowly, I feel my body being filled by a delicious sense of peace. I find myself thinking of the two biggest loves of my life and discover myself smiling. I am so grateful for my daughter, who has grown into a beautiful woman, and my dear and serene Eli, my road companion and my loyal partner who will join me soon to start a new adventure. Eli and Mariana, always together, always independent at the same time.
Eli, the one who provided me with security and balance since the moment I landed in Canada. I was a successful entrepreneur and outstanding marketer

with no savings. My financial management skills sucked. Eli was on the opposite side of the spectrum. His strong administration and financial skills and his discipline acquired during his army years, allowed him to pay off his house, have a retirement plan in place and have savings for his daughter's future academic education while working as a taxi driver. We were opposites that attracted creating a harmonic and balanced team.

I am happily surprised by the realization that I am dreaming again.

I dream of seeing people doing what they long for and enjoying the freedom to choose their own destinies.

I would like to whisper in everyone's ear that there is *nothing* to fear, that the only thing that may not have a solution is death, and all the rest can be fixed. Life has taught me that no matter what we do or stop doing, sooner or later, one way or another, inevitably, death will arrive.

I know that it's totally okay to fall and start again as many times as needed. We can fail, and it is okay because the most important thing is the journey.

I would like to proclaim that by giving generously without expecting anything in return, one's life becomes richer. If we all lived this way, there would always be someone around the corner giving their gift to the world and each one of us would receive what we need, without limits.

I've learned through the years that nature is wise and holds all the answers we are looking for. It has an order and a unique agenda. Humans have no control over it, although we would like to think we do.

The story you just read, is an invitation to rediscover with me all that there is to be learned in the time we have left to live. Each day opens an opportunity to expand our horizons and to abandon the fears that paralyze us and make us dubious. It is also a call for us to realize that every human being who crosses our path presents a new opportunity for self-knowledge and wisdom, because behind every face there is a unique and unrepeatable history.

I would like to remind all of us that time is the most valuable commodity nowadays although it is the most uncontrollable gift we have. We cannot buy it or sell it. We cannot stop it or go back. The moments enjoyed are stamps in our memory and dye our hearts with warmth for eternity. Are you aware that we are all collections of memories? It is only up to us to create as many new experiences as possible to treasure for life.

Not to advance is to retreat, because the river continues its course.

Say YES, Ask questions later

Changes are difficult but never impossible when they are met with patience, tenacity and discipline. For all situations there is more than one path that will lead to the destination. Just as the ice thaws and its waters follow the known path, when something blocks its way, the water dredges and erodes the blockage until it creates a new pathway so it can continue flowing.

Failure is the true route to learning. Whoever fails the most, becomes wiser and less fearful at each turn.

Why not cooperate instead of competing with each other? Community and solidarity are underrated powers.

This is an invitation to live NOW. Leave nothing for tomorrow, because tomorrow, well what is tomorrow? Maybe it does not even exist!

I challenge you to cry hard and laugh harder, to get wet under the rain and feel the drops running down your face. Let's play at discovering shapes in the clouds and smile when we see a bird bathing in a pond. I urge you to sing, paint, plant, write and scribble.

I would especially like to ask you to tell your own story. Each one of us is a book waiting to be written, or told, like the fables that were told to us when we were kids. We are all part of the history of the world with lessons to learn, and discoveries to share.

I wrote my story with the hope that my wanderings around the world and the landscapes I painted in this book will inspire hearts that have not yet been given the privilege and joy of living with true freedom.

Dare to say "Yes" and ask questions later!

Say YES, Ask questions later

ABOUT THE AUTHOR

Mariana Konsolos

Mariana moved to Canada with hardly any English skills. Struggling with acceptance, and while establishing a romantic relationship with an intriguing man, she had to keep moving forward.

It was hard to accept the Mariana who existed in Uruguay, had vanished when she set foot in Canada.

Soon she understood she had two options: to complain and feel miserable, or to find a solution. She chose to see that time as a gift, an opportunity.

"I felt I was given a plain canvas, a bunch of colors, and time to paint a new life, a new version of myself."

Her entrepreneurial spirit and transferable skills helped her to build success this time through her talent with fashion accessories, creating a loyal community of women.

Say YES, Ask questions later

Did you learn something from the book? Please share what you learned when you leave a review on Amazon.

Would you like to stay in touch and learn more about the VIP Book Club?
Facebook.com/marianakonsolos
Linkedin.com/in/marianakonsolos
Instagram.com/marianakonsolos
www.marianakonsolos.com/say-yes-ask-questions-later

Manufactured by Amazon.ca
Bolton, ON

20056559R00116